MW00618506

PRAISE FOR *TOWARD AFRODIASPORIC AND AFROFUTURIST PHILOSOPHIES OF RELIGION*

"*Toward Afrodiasporic and Afrofuturist Philosophies of Religion* is an imaginative and illuminating must-read primer for anyone interested in indigenous religious philosophies. The volume offers a compelling challenge to well-worn Eurocentric approaches to and presuppositions about 'religion.' Burgeoning fields like hip hop spirituality and controversial viewpoints on gender/sexuality are reappraised through a decolonial lens. The array of assembled essays signal, perhaps more importantly, the long-lasting vitality of the ancestors on present-day scholarship."

—ROY WHITAKER
Associate Professor of Religious Studies, San Diego State University

"This book is a remarkable model for interrogating Eurocentric theories with expansive understandings of religion and a deep grounding in aesthetics, experience, and Africana philosophies. Each essay breaks open and constructs new ways of understanding both Africana culture, its own self-understanding, and the unique way art harnesses hope. This book includes crucial ideas for anyone interested in philosophy of religion, aesthetics, or Afrofuturism."

—MONICA A. COLEMAN
Professor of Africana Studies, University of Delaware

"Jon Ivan Gill is the philosopher of religion many of us need for the twenty-first century. Here, Gill's innovation and courageous experimentation shines as he gives voice to the often unheard—the young, those from historically marginalized groups, and those who espouse and sustain the rich legacy of Black thought. Contributing to the ongoing conversations about Afrofuturism and its relationship to religion, Gill curates a fine set of essays useful for new and seasoned philosophers of religion alike."

—CHRISTOPHER DRISCOLL
Assistant Professor of Religion Studies, Lehigh University

Toward Afrodiasporic and Afrofuturist Philosophies of Religion

Toward Afrodiasporic and Afrofuturist Philosophies of Religion

Edited by
JON IVAN GILL

Foreword by
YTASHA L. WOMACK

WIPF & STOCK · Eugene, Oregon

TOWARD AFRODIASPORIC AND AFROFUTURIST PHILOSOPHIES
OF RELIGION

Wipf & Stock
An Imprint of Wipf and Stock Publishers
199 W. 8th Ave., Suite 3
Eugene, OR 97401

www.wipfandstock.com

PAPERBACK ISBN: 978-1-7252-5276-9
HARDCOVER ISBN: 978-1-7252-5277-6
EBOOK ISBN: 978-1-7252-5278-3

04/13/22

Contents

Contents

Ytasha L. Womack

Foreword
Which Way is New?

WHEN I WROTE *AFROFUTURISM: The World of Black Sci-Fi & Fanta-sy Culture,* I was thinking about my friends in college, all of whom were discussing Afrofuturist ideas on a never-ending hunt to con-nect the threads of music, time, and memory. They, and I for that matter, combed through hip-hop lyrics, samples, loops, historical treaties, theories, and narratives, to uncover the patterns that spoke to our higher selves—a spiraled ladder to deeper revelation and liberation. My first conversation on Afrofuturism was with a fellow student at Clark Atlanta University's campus and we found kin-ship in a speculative bridge of song lyrics, history, and time theory. Metaphysics and its philosophies were our shared foundation. That conversation was one of many that would come to define my col-lege years. For that reason, I'm delighted that my book has found resonance and was a reference to help the students featured in this collection find truths that speak to an idealized future.

So much about how we discuss futures is a discourse on movement. How do I get there? Here, where I stand, is the ques-tion. There, where I'm going, is where the answer lies. Sometimes, that journey is the answer. *Towards an Afrodiasporic Afrofuturist Philosophy of Religion* is the onset of a quest. One's life is always a meditation or testament to a wealth of beliefs. How does that quest change when the destination is a philosophy of religion?

I grew up in a New Thought philosophy in a church community where Afrofuturist ideas (they weren't calling it that, of course) were valued. Although the New Thought experience isn't a rare experience, it's certainly unique to be cognizant as a child that one is engaging with a philosophy that could be discussed within and beyond Christian frameworks and personal identities. The approach was universalist and aspirational, with frequent parallels made to Buddhism. Although, in the spiritual institution I grew up in, the beliefs weren't presented in the context of African religions or aligning with this approach, its philosophical malleability made incorporating or understanding African spiritual approaches for ones entrenched in a Western Judeo-Christian lens easier. However, such approaches were also made easy because of my lifelong love affair with arts, music, and dance. I was immersed in Black Chicago culture and its house and soul music offshoots. Hip-hop's explosion, birthed in the Bronx, came to define my era, adopted by corporations as the ultimate marketing tool to reach a generation while serving as a compelling commentary on postmodernism and youth identity; this urban, Midwestern, post-Great-Migration, late-twentieth-century life of performing with Black dance schools and multiethnic high schools before heading off to a Historically Black University in Atlanta where regional and international Black music, culture, and practices collided and rediscovered one another. Conversations aside, my practical experience with African philosophy and Afrofuturism came through immersion in a widening sea of Black cultures across the Americas and beyond, because philosophies carried across the ocean and fused in the kiln of duress are often alive in elements of Black artforms and ways of being. The whispers of all times speak even when the discourse around it escapes those who embody it.

One is not always in an environment where they can freely explore Afrofuturism, or African Diaspora philosophy free of religious dogma or a hierarchical gaze while navigating Western spaces. One is not always in a space where such contemplations are valued or where such ideas can be informed with insights and histories. Some find the discourse in classrooms. Others find the conversation through music, art shows, literature, barbershops, or among friends with a shared love of comics or quantum physics. Some find it within religious institutions. The sparks that lead to epiphanies vary. As many of the writers in this class anthology note, the points of exploration uncovering the basis for a philosophy are scattered across cultural touchstones and cultural production; entrenched in music, art, and method. Despite Afrofuturist and African philosophy being prevalent in Black cultural production everywhere, Western framing isn't always adept at articulating its language and tapestry. Yet, classes devoted to thinking on these ideas are happening in greater frequency.

Many of the essays in this book use song lyrics or music artists and their artistic worldviews as a starting point for their inquiry. Some look to gender and identity, their relationship to hip-hop, hip-hop's positionality, or frustration with space inspirations as a starting point. Those who study religion may find these to be curious beginnings for uncovering a philosophy. Yet, inherent in these perspectives is a way of being which the writers contemplate.

Writing works while on the path of evolving thought is always an interesting marker of time. As a writer, I can sense many of the contributors looking to their relationship to Afrofuturism and African Diasporic philosophy through the practices of others. Who am I in the Afrodiasporic, Afrofuturist paradigm? What do these connections mean? Why do I find cultural memory and threads to futures in Afrobeat's Fela Kuti, gospel rap, the priestess energy of Erykah Badu, or the storied dreams of Travis Scott? What is my philosophy towards the future? An Afrofuture? How does my philosophy of life shape religion and vice versa? How do I or the works I'm drawn to shape Afrofuturist Afrodiasporic paradigms? Although these essays are not about the student writers per se, in another sense it is an exploration of their curiosities, liberation dreams, and frustrations.

The works in this book are markers of thought for this class of writers, all of whom were ignited by the notions of new futures and an excitement about unearthing philosophies in cultural practices and music in the African Diaspora. Some grappled with

Afrofuturist ideas for the first time. How the process of writing these essays will impact each writer's worldview in the future is yet to be seen. However, the value of classes such as the one that gave rise to this compilation is that they provide space/time for students to rework ideas. Without the introduction of new works, the dialogue between fellow students and teachers, many of these ideas could've remained in the student's subconscious, tickling their conscious, but rarely taking form. I wrote *Afrofuturism* so that students could build on these ideas. Examining futures and culture from an African Diasporic lens is forever normalized after class experiences like the ones the writers in this anthology were a part of. The students in this book will likely always be on the hunt for more works and beliefs, past and present, from the African Diaspora and elsewhere, that shape, or can shape, an inspired future/now.

Jon Ivan Gill

Acknowledgements

First off, to my maternal grandmother, Lessie Alaine McDonald Turner Sayles, this is for you. You showed me the blues, the foundation for Afrofuturism, not only in your radio, but in your life. Gratitude for raising me like you did. Shout to the '68 Chevy Chevelle jalopy.

Also, to my paternal Aunt Florence Maud Thompson, I'm indebted to you for your role as mentor, confidant, historian, and example. Your role as matriarch of the family was heaven on earth, and we still float within your greatness. We feel you in the pages of this work.

Steve and Sharon Andrews, your lives are a testament to what committed love can achieve. You both are always there to listen and offer wisdom, without which I would be loose sheets of papers wasted to the wind. Respect!

Mom and Dad, you already know. Let's say it again. Your influence is unquestioned and essential. Muchas gracias!

All of my family who weren't mentioned, you just were. I don't want to hear any foolishness from ANY of you on this! Laugh at that, please. Much love to you all.

Acknowledgements

José Francisco Morales Torres, Raphael Reyes, Itzpapolotl x Huizitzilin, Robert C. Saler, Roy Whitaker, Monica A. Coleman, Ytasha Womack, Tomorrow Kings, Michael Adame, Avenida del Roble, Philip Butler, Girim Jung, James Howard Hill, Callid Keefe-Perry, Philip Clayton, Roland Faber, Tony Hoshaw, Scott Holland, Jonathan Calvillo, Christopher M. Driscoll, Monica R. Miller, Daniel White Hodge, Elonda Clay, Vitor Westhelle, Jeff Cervantez, José Sentmanat, Dominique Hitchcock, David Stewart, Jon Stone, Gabriel Estrada, Peter Lowentrout, Maisha Handy, M Adryael Tong, Vanessa Lovelace, Anna Case-Winters, Deborah Mullen, Ken Sawyer, Robert Brawley, Jane Brawley, Katie Snipes Lancaster, Maria Jackson, Tataduhende, Chicago Hip-Hop, Joshua Brown, Peg O'Conner, Lisa Heldke, Tommy Valentini, Janine Genelin, Center for Process Studies, Gustavus Adolphus College, Patrick Reyes, the Claremont Colleges and all other lures that inspired what you will read, thank you for your co-authorship of the text that will never be fully written, as the stream never stays still enough to be ossified.

Peace.

Jon Ivan Gill

Introduction

Toward Afrodiasporic and Afrofuturist
Philosophies of Religion

THIS TRULY WAS AN experiment. An experiment that I semi-expected to go nowhere. But I should have hoped for more, as much more that I could have ever expected is what we got.

During the school semester of 2018–2019, I was fortunate to gain a visiting professorship at Pomona College in the area of Africana Studies in Religion/Africana Philosophy of Religion. As I was reading the job call, I was thrown off as well as pleasantly surprised. Maybe I was naïve (I actually wasn't), but I didn't know there was a such thing as "Africana philosophy of religion." Such phraseology is nothing that the academy has either espoused or even made a serious live option in the academic study of religion or philosophy. In many instances, philosophy of religion as it is taught in colleges and universities in the United States and globally derives its foci from questions that arise from Western theisms, questions that quite often are incapable of encompassing the complexities and multiplicities found in traditions that share few or no similarities with Western theisms shaped from (even though they may take quasi-religious and secular forms) Judeo-Christian practices and understandings. Due to the structure of Enlightenment-derived philosophies of religion in the vain of Kant, Schelling, Hegel, and

Schleiermacher (which in many instances only consider as a foot-note to the reflections on the same or similar questions of thinkers from India, China, Egypt, Ethiopia, Mexico, and more), are these frameworks capable of analyzing the ways in which religious be-lief is both defined and at work in Rastafari, the Moorish Science Temple of America, Afrofuturist art, Santería, and Hip-Hop? If the answer to this question is "No," then how do we adequately discuss/account for/critically engage the religiosity of these life-transforma-tive methods of existence in the world in a philosophy of religion sort of midset? Is that even possible?

I know that my "before is behind," to draw from my father's Belizean Kriol. I've used the beginning as a semi-conclusion. But all will come together shortly. And I'd better hurry. This is an intro, and I don't have much time.

The Religious Studies department at Pomona graciously al-lowed me to assemble my own curriculum for my visiting year. I used this opportunity to approach within the setting of the class-room some far-reaching combinations of ideas I'd wanted to ex-plore on fertile grounds. Some of the course titles were "Hip-Hop as an Afrodiasporic Religious Practice," "Aesthetic Religious Atheism of the Darker Hues," and "Electronic Music and Meaning." During the fall semester, I taught the class that bears the name of this edited volume, "Toward Afrodiasporic and Afrofuturist Philosophies of Religion," in which the students and I studied the discipline of phi-losophy of religion alongside African philosophies and Afrofuturist works. What emerged from this was a remarkably novel semester-long discussion on the richness of Afrodiasporic philosophical and Afrofuturist materials and the communities that develop from them as religions and religious.

The class of thirteen students began with a working/reworking definition of religion for some of us. We chose not to adopt a more narrow understanding that in some sense includes belief in liter-ally transcendent ideas of deities and mandates of conduct which emerge in the empirical world from suprarational positions. Rather, we chose to take the approach of sociology of religion, lived experi-ence, and history, referring to religion (*religio*= "to bind") as any-thing which provides meaning to an individual or group of people, thus sustaining the individual or community through a binding to a way of life they commit to which makes sense of the world. For the purposes of the class, religion is a decision to anchor oneself to an ideology amidst a world where meaning itself is arbitrary: it is literally the human "making a way out of no way,"[1] as process philosopher of religion Monica A. Coleman would say. The first few days with this vibrant, scholarly, and plain fun group of students were a shift of perspective for many of them: some of them remarked that their views of religion before these days only related the term to Christianity, Islam, Judaism, or other belief systems commonly thought of as religious. Now, the playing field for exploration was wide open. From this unstable foundation (I'm always skeptical when a foundation is too secure), we could look at Afrodiasporic philosophy and Afrofuturism as religious and religions, and ask if philosophy of religion as it has stood historically in the Western canon could engage the religiosity the class, even at this early stage, was sure it possessed.

With such an understanding of religion (which is of course not new, but maybe our application of it is somewhat novel), I began to invite the students to consider aesthetic and cultural productions of the Afrodiaspora not commonly associated with the world religions as religions not in need of any sort of tradition generally accepted as religious to give them any religiosity. In discussions on religion and the arts, the tendency in many instances seems to be to try to find traces of an "accepted" world religion in a work of art as opposed to acknowledging the work of art as religious on its own, whether it contains an idea of deities or not. The corpus of the work of Monica R. Miller has cautioned us against such a starting point, suggesting that to begin searching for recognizable elements of what many call religion by default is to ignore the religiosity that works of art and aesthetic schools of thought possess in themselves. Religion comes from somewhere, and insofar as Afrodiasporic works of art such as the Afrofuturist poetry and mixed media of Chicago's Krista Franklin, the global subverse of Hip-Hop philosophies articulated and enacted by the Wu-Tang Clan, and the science fiction of Octavia

---

1. Coleman, *Making a Way Out of No Way*.

Butler imagine, and invite us into imagining, new ways to exist in the world (something essential for elongated survival), they are participating in the same strand of the *creation* of meaning that we sometimes forget is occurring in the world religions some view as being sacred and otherworldly. Grounding my own work in my recently released book on underground rap and process philosophy and process theology entitled *Underground Rap as Religion: A Theopoetic Examination of a Process Aesthetic Religion* (Routledge, 2019 hardcover. 2021 paperback) is a term I use called "Aesthetic Religion." Aesthetic Religion asserts that works of art and schools of aesthetic thought provide the adherent similar types of meaning as world religions provide to those who follow them.[2]

This brings us to a serious dilemma. Can philosophy of religion, a discipline that gains its name from the late and post-Enlightenment discussions of continental thinkers such as Hegel, Kant, Spinoza, Hume, Schelling, Kierkegaard, and even Nietzsche, address the kinds of belief systems that appear in the types of Aesthetic Religions that we've discussed? This question goes beyond the initial query of discerning the adequacy of philosophy of religion to address the religiosity of Aesthetic Religions. Here, we are asking a question about the ability of Western philosophy of religion approaches to adequately reverence some Aesthetic Religions due to their origins in non-European sources. What the hell would Kant really do with the serious assertion that Afrodiasporic and Afrofuturist art is a religion, especially when he does not allow for Afrodiasporic people to be considered as equal to Europeans on the human scale, let alone hold any systems of aesthetic and cultural products *created* by them to anchor their worlds as worthy of the designation "religion?" The rituals of Obeah, the ring shout of the Afrodiasporic US church conjured from the past during chattel slavery, the rhythms and soul of salsa, the addictive kick-snare

2. See Brent Nongbri, *Before Religion: A History of a Modern Concept* (New Haven: Yale University Press, 2015) for a short and robust treatment of the problematic and Eurocentric reductions of the traditions we now know as the "world religions." Nongbri asserts that colonization via Christianity is the normative mold against which all other religious traditions are judged and caricaturized by. I found his insights very useful in the development of deconstructive and reconstructive strategies for the foundation of the class.

of 90's boom-bap—all things that have liberated the diaspora and the world—are outside of the scope of the word "religion" in "philosophy of religion" as shaped by the Western philosophical world. Monica R. Miller and Christopher M. Driscoll hold that

> Another/an *Other* orientation could suggest black religion is an oxymoron, in that "religion" is the totem of the odd confederation of tribes known as white Europeans, And the history of religions (and its comparative approach) is the making of white European identity through the ongoing questioning of the rest of the world's similarities to white European identity. Yet, these possibilities are shaped by the concern over the object of religion, not over distance making via method.[3]

The students, while finding great use for many of the categories utilized in philosophy of religion such as questions around the existence of God, miracles, religious pluralism, the problem of evil, gendered ideas of the divine, and other subjects/questions, seemed to agree with Driscoll and Miller: the thing we call philosophy of religion not only intentionally overlooks, but also makes invisible, the very means of existing in the world that the diaspora has thrived off of, pre- and postcolonization. Its formulations of these questions asked centuries before the advent of the Enlightenment are hierarchical, racist, classist, and elitist. The aim of philosophy of religion—the investigation of the nature of religious belief itself—is a worthy pursuit in itself. But the students were unanimous in asserting that the things now included in our definition of religion were beyond the scope of philosophy of religion as it stands. Maybe we could forge toward new ways to seriously investigate the inner workings of these religious traditions through language, strategies, and thinking that wouldn't perform reductionist violence on their richness.

In an attempt to approach philosophy of religion from the concerns of the Afrodiaspora, I saw a need to serve as a tour guide through the discipline of what has been called "African philosophy." My personal hunch was and is that African philosophy, especially

3. Driscoll and Miller, *Method as Identity*, 17 (emphasis original).

negritude, the work of Theophilus Okere, John Mbiti, Jennifer Vest, bell hooks, and other profound thinkers are philosophies of religions themselves, whether or not their writing engages explicit and/or literal notions of God or other concerns of the philosophy of religion. According to the sociological/constructive definition of "religion" the class agreed upon, given the fact that the corpus of African philosophy from text to oral tradition to daily practice is a compilation of strategies to live and flourish in the world in the most dynamic and intense ways possible (what I would similarly call *centers of significance* in Aesthetic Religion), it has a religiosity that is both religious and religions. African philosophy is a natural organization of the world that perpetually ingresses and redistributes to a context that which is most important to it, similar to Alfred North Whitehead's notion of God in *Process and Reality*, or maybe more appropriately Sanaa Lathan as Syndey's description of Hip-Hop in *Love and Hip-Hop*. Guided by the thought of philosopher Barry Hallen, we asked questions around when African philosophy began, is there something intrinsic, nonnegotiable, and essentially "African" about African philosophy (ethnophilosophy), was there a time in which African philosophy did not exist and had to be brought on the scene (professional philosophy), and whether or not African philosophy is solely derived from an assumption about the people who may be articulating or practicing the thought/ways of life (similar to Belgian thinker Placide Tempel's *Bantu Philosophy*, which asserted and implied that Africa had a singular distinct way of thinking philosophically) or from the perpetually changing existential situation from which the thought emerges (focusing on the hermeneutical approach that many thinkers who identify as African philosophers find valuable in Gadamer, Heidegger, Husserl, and Sartre).[4] In this mode, we began to ask contextual questions around the connections between twentieth-century African philosophy and meaning-making in the present for the Afrodiaspora from the United States to Puerto Rico, and found more satisfying methods of engaging these religious questions here than through

4. Serequeberhan, 5,9.

Western philosophy of religion (which we studied alongside African philosophy).

This class owes a great debt to the work of Jennifer Vest, who in the article "The Promise of Caribbean Philosophy: How It Can Contribute to a New Dialogic in Philosophy," provides a way for non "Western" philosophical thinkers to dialogue amongst themselves without the philosophical traditions of Britain, France, and Germany (among others) serving as both mediator and measuring stick of what is "proper" philosophical dialogue. The method encourages dialogue amidst non-Western thinkers without the expectation of convincing someone with a divergent view of your own. Rather, through intense discussion, parties are forced to examine problematic points in their own positions while finding better ways of implementing plausible ones. I feel that this class was one that decentered Europe as the pinnacle of philosophical discourse, with most of the conversations on philosophy of religion in the course revolving around rappers, poets, singers, and film directors who identified as being part of the diaspora. Instead of attempting to synthesize the discussions around Western notions found in philosophy of religion, we did our own thing, basing questions and answers (many times peripherally) about the problem of evil, the existence of God, religious language, and religious pluralism (or the lack thereof) on the cultural norms and contextual concerns that we brought to the class via our own flesh. There were many times where these questions didn't even come up. If Kendrick Lamar or Rapsody are deities, the conversation about whether or not they exist may be unnecessary (unless we are embarking on a journey in philosophy of mind or epistemology). What effects do these deities and some type of belief in them have on the world might be a more adequate question, but a Jamesian type of analysis from *The Varieties of Religious Experience* or Wach's *Sociology of Religion* may fail at addressing the effects of religious belief in relation to human figures not expressly connected to a confessional religion, a realm in which belief takes on a different form than it does in Hip-Hop. I could go on. The point is that Vest's take on Caribbean philosophy opened up a conversational format for me to employ to ensure that European categories and voices did not serve as the main interlocutors on which we moved toward Afrodiasporic and Afrofuturist philosophies of religion.

One of the most important and most exciting parts of the class was its Afrofuturist dimension. My hire at Pomona came after the end of the 2018 spring semester, a point when most students had already registered for classes. Mid-August, Erin Runions, then Department Chair of Religious Studies, informed me that "Toward Afrodiasporic and Afrofuturist Philosophies of Religion" had quite a small number of students enrolled and that it might need to be canceled. At the suggestion of Professor Runions, I went into self-promotional Hip-Hop MC mode, took up some Afrofuturist art, and devised a flyer for the course. This is the sort of "get the word out quickly" flare you learn from years of pounding the pavement in the creative underground scenes of Chicago. Within a few days of the flyer going out, the class filled. Now, it was time to really get busy.

My work with the Chicago collective Tomorrow Kings has been described by many (including esteemed Afrofuturist Krista Franklin) as a type of Afrofuturism, and I think a good amount of my solo releases as Gilead7 between 2003–2009 flow in the same river. What is Afrofuturism? Good question. There are several definitions that have been attached to it, coming from Mark Dery, Alondra Nelson, Ytasha Womack, and other important thinkers. Drawing from all of these definitions, the class seemed to reside within the region of describing Afrofuturism as thinking about the possibilities of identities of the Afrodiasporic self in ways that not only disregard but also deconstruct and defy the methods in which Afrodiasporic people have been forced by the aftershocks of White supremacy to identify. Many Afrofuturist science fiction writers seem to suggest that Afrodiasporic people will only be free in a future where the systemic structures of oppression no longer exist or never existed. The work of Octavia Butler, Erykah Badu, Sun Ra, Jimi Hendrix, Edgardo Miranda-Rodriguez, and Noname were points of encounter with Afrofuturist ways of thinking, thinking that challenged us to reimagine gender, race, class, sexual orientation, ableism, nationalism, and other facets of identity politics/building through our own Afrofuturist religious lenses. Throughout the semester, we stuck close to Ytasha Womack's *Afrofuturism: The World of Black Sci-Fi and Fantasy Culture* as we studied Afrofuturist ways of becoming (Whitehead) as religions and religious, and attempted to do meta-work, forging possible flexible and unstable categories that an Afrodiasporic and Afrofuturist philosophy of religion might use to examine belief at such unique levels.

So, this collection of wonderful papers is, in many ways, a shot in the dark which will prove most successful if its aim is not reached. We attempted to move seriously toward possible Afrodiasporic and Afrofuturist philosophies of religion in the close of the class, as the final assignment was for students to: 1) discuss what ingredients would be essential to an Afrodiasporic or Afrofuturist philosophy of religion, 2) Identify what sort of categories (if any) should be designed to group the phenomena and ways of thought/life we encountered, and 3) how they would propose an Afrodiasporic or Afrofuturist philosophy of religion that would serve the traditions in question more efficiently than the methods historically used by philosophers of religion for very different data. I'm not sure if we achieved that at all. However, through vibrant, tenuous, and difficult discussions, writing, listening, clowning (shout out to Vicki Hirales, former Coordinator of Pomona College's Philosophy and Religious Studies departments, who had an office right across the hall from the class and put up with us when we just took a break from the rigor to just be our silly, loud, and free selves), and openness to seriously interrogate and reimagine the categories of philosophy of religion, African philosophy, and Afrofuturism, we give you these offerings to play through.

Utter gratitude goes to Madisen Barre-Hemingway (Pitzer College), Dray Denson (Pomona College), Nathan Hahn (Pomona College), Elijah Jabbar-Bey (Pomona College), Kalanzi Kalibwani Kajubi (Pitzer College), Justin Lennox (Pomona College), Benjamin Miller (Pitzer College), Rachel Murdock (Pomona College), Magali Ngouabou (Pomona College), Olu Omoyugbo (Pomona College), Desiree Rawls (Pitzer College), and Daniel Savin (Pomona College). All of you made this experience indelible, and I hope this text, your text, generates for the reader the dynamic energy we conjured from the ancestors in our modern, hush-harbor meetings, where we, through ancient sorcery, syncretized philosophy of religion, African philosophy, and Afrofuturism. To Erin Runions, Zhiru Ng, Jerry Irish, Zayn Kassam, Oona Eisenstadt, and Darryl Smith, thank you for allowing me to return to the Claremont Colleges a couple years after completing my doctoral work at Claremont Graduate University. I am grateful that you added me to the faculty of Pomona College and allowed me to experiment alongside you in the Religious Studies department for the 2018–2019 school year. Through one-on-one conversations, reading groups, and living amongst you all in community, I learned valuable lessons about the field and about being a human. You truly made me feel welcome and valued. This one is for you.

Continue. You won't hear from me anymore. And that's probably the best thing about this text.

REFERENCES

Coleman, Monica. *Making a Way Out of No Way: A Womanist Theology.* Minneapolis: Fortress, 2008.

Driscoll, Christopher M., and Monica R. Miller. *Method as Identity: Manufacturing Distance in the Academic Study of Religion.* Lanham, MD: Lexington, 2018.

Nongbri, Brent. *Before Religion: A History of a Modern Concept.* New Haven: Yale University Press, 2015.

Serequeberhan, Tsenay. *The Hermeneutics of African Philosophy: Horizon and Discourse.* New York: Routledge, 1994.

Dray Densen

Transing Southern Cartographies: An Incommensurable Win

Black Christian Theology and the Blackness of Gender

INTRODUCTION TO AN INTERVENTION

A comprehensive November 2017 survey by the Human Rights Campaign and the Trans People of Color Coalition finds that eighty-eight of at least 102 victims of fatal anti-trans and trans-misogynist violence between 2013 to mid-November 2017 were women; eighty-seven were trans people of color (TPOC), and of those eighty-seven lives, at least seventy-five were Black.[1] These identities clearly intersect: of the known twenty-eight trans lives lost in 2017, twenty-one were Black transgender people, and of those, at least twenty were known and self-identifying Black trans-feminine people or trans women.[2] The reports, by nature

1. McBride, "Alarming Report," para. 5.

2. Roberts, "2017 US Trans Murders List," para. 8. Roberts's list does not include, or was compiled before, reports on the 2017 deaths of Brandi Seals, Jaylow McGlory, Brooklyn Breyanna Stevenson, Scout Schultz, Sean Hake, and Kiwi Herring. Seals, McGlory, Stevenson, and Herring were Black trans women.

of circumstances, cannot or cannot yet count all victims of fatal trans-antagonism due to misgendering by family, state forces, and presently undiscovered violence.

There must be specific attention to, and alarm in, the South: the 2017 Human Rights Campaign (HRC) and the Transgender People of Color Coalition (TPOCC) report identifies the South as the space wherein 55 percent of trans murders were committed, "including 16 of the 25 victims reported so far in [November] 2017."[3] Violence against Black trans people, especially Black trans women and femmes, is endemic; the fact of Black trans death being majorly situated within the South is no footnote, and from this epidemic arises a need for mappings, interrogations, and contestations of the necropolitical systems/apparatuses that produce Black trans death.[4]

In his seminal text, *a Black Theology of Liberation,* departed ancestor James Cone leads with this: "There can be no Christian ideology that is not identified unreservedly with those who are humiliated and abused."[5] Cone dedicated his life, body, and energy to not simply inscribing Christianity and Christian theology with Blackness, but by emphasizing that God himself is Black. He makes clear that those aligned with Christian theology must be aligned with the obliteration of whiteness, the affirmation of Blackness, and the obliteration of all oppressive entanglements related to racial capitalism and systems of anti-Blackness. He emphasizes that, "anyone who claims to be fighting against the problem of oppression

3. Human Rights Campaign and Trans People of Color Coalition, *Time to Act,* 35.

4. I borrow Achille Mbembe's concept of *necropolitics* to contextualize the endemic of Black trans death within the State. That all of the reports used—the only available and comprehensive reports—are derived from non-profit, independent, and/or local news sources speaks to the death and obscuration that has been projected onto Black trans lives. That multiple lists, ranging from twenty to thirty *known* names of Black trans death, coincides with a December 2017 order from the White House that requires the CDC to abstain from mentioning the very identity (in conjunction with their Blackness) for which these people were killed—*transgender*—also contextualizes the historic erasure that has been projected onto Black trans bodies. See also, Sun and Eilperin, "CDC Gets List of Forbidden Words."

5. Cone, *Black Theology of Liberation,* 1.

and does not analyze the exploitive role of capitalism is either naive or an agent of the enemies of freedom."[6]

Published by Orbis Books in 1970, *A Black Theology of Liberation* emerges as a powerful and meditative text on the conditions of possibility for Black bodies on Earth, and for theology as a vehicle for change *only* when it its imbued within Blackness and Black liberation. In a May 2008 interview with Michael Powell of the *New York Times*, Cone described, allow[ing] himself a chuckle, [that] "[One] might say we took our Christianity from Martin and our emphasis on Blackness from Malcolm."[7] His proximity to Malcolm's fiery polemics, and his mandate of Black liberation, are inalienable. In the preface to the 1986 edition of *A Black Theology of Liberation,* Cone describes his urgency in producing his text in the nexus of the Civil Rights Movement that led to the rise of the Black Power Movement in the 1970s and 80s. Cone remembers:

> Again Malcolm expressed what I felt deep within my being: The time that we're living in, now is not an era where one who is oppressed is looking toward the oppressor to give him some system or form of logic or reason. What is logical to the oppressor isn't logical to the oppressed. And what is reason to the oppressor isn't reason to the oppressed.[8]

Cone brilliantly rails against, as he later terms, conservative and passive acceptance of white supremacy, as articulated by many Black preachers in the time preceding and during his writing, and violent shows of power by white bodies. The first few pages of Cone's text contain an indictment of the violence of white theology and its intentional failings of Black bodies, of the ways in which it has assisted in the bondage of Black bodies: "Throughout the history of this country, from the Puritans to the death-of-God theologians, the theological problems treated in white churches and theological

---

6. Cone, *Black Theology of Liberation,* xvii.

7. Cone, as quoted in Powell, "Fiery Theology Under Fire," para. 16.

8. Cone, *Black Theology of Liberation,* 1.

schools are defined in such a manner that they are unrelated to the problem of being Black in a white, racist society."[9]

In a passionate language that hopes to spark Black revelation itself, Cone protests the total obfuscation of anti-Blackness, racial capitalism, and colonialism that allowed white theology power over Black bodies:

> When I thought about the long history of Black suffering and the long silence of white theologians in its regard, I could not always control my pen or my tongue. I did not feel that I should in any way be accountable to white theologians or their cultural etiquette. It was not a time to be polite but rather a time to speak the truth with love, courage, and care for the masses of Blacks.[10]

In the text, Cone does not censor himself—and rightly so—and in keeping the fullness of his language, which is laden with terms that white bodies could consider derogatory, he positions his work as fully and unabashedly committed to the freeing of Black bodies from systemic and theological chains that are tethered to the structure of whiteness. Cone grounds his work in materiality, reminding that "[a]lthough God is the intended subject of theology, God does not do theology. *Human beings do theology*."[11] He disrupts the colonial tradition of white slaveholders, theologians, and white bodies in general that includes the practice of distancing violence enacted against Black and brown bodies as "God's will." White bodies have actively constructed systems of white theology that have and were designed to delimit the movement of Black bodies, which he argues Black bodies can and must attempt to disrupt for their survival and at the recognition of their beauty.[12]

Cone also indicts white theologians' emphasis on peace as a means of condemning and attempting to assuage Black rage and revolution. Writes Cone:

---

9. Cone, *Black Theology of Liberation*, 9.

10. Cone, *Black Theology of Liberation*, xix.

11. Cone, *Black Theology of Liberation*, xix (emphasis original).

12. Cone, *Black Theology of Liberation*, 15.

> White appeals to "wait and talk it over" are irrelevant when children are dying and men and women are being tortured. We will not let whitey cool this one with his pious love ethic but will seek to enhance our hostility, bringing it to its full manifestation. Black survival is at stake here, and we Blacks must define and assert the conditions necessary for our being-in-the-world.[13]

As evidenced in his writing, Cone condemns how whiteness and white Christian theology have revoked the ontology and autonomy of Black bodies by assigning them to a paradigm of being-for-Other, *being the Other*, as opposed to being-for-Self. Cone professes that a white God is inherently to the threat of Black being; a white God or Jesus places Black bodies in proximity to annihilation; to nonbeing. He writes that: "Black theology must realize that the white Jesus has no place in the Black community, and it is our task to destroy him. We must replace him with the Black messiah, as Albert Cleage would say, a messiah who sees his existence as inseparable from Black liberation and the destruction of white racism."[14]

Because white supremacy exists, Cone cites that omnipotence does not function in a way that allows for its complete obliteration by God. Because God is Black, was oppressed, and is aligned with Black suffering, the dismantling of whiteness as a system is a protracted effort that must happen by Black bodies, and bodies aligned with Black struggle and liberation, through any means necessary here on Earth. Cone writes: "Omnipotence does not refer to God's absolute power to accomplish what God wants. As John Macquarrie says, omnipotence is 'the power to let something stand out from nothing and to be.'"[15] Theodicy exists, which is why Black theology must be Black liberation theology, which is inherently concerned with the obliteration of white supremacist paradigms that hold Blackness back from complete and total liberation.

Departed ancestor Cone also eschews white, liberal, gradual, and capitalist notions of "winning" that evade true, tangible

---

13. Cone, *Black Theology of Liberation*, 12.
14. Cone, *Black Theology of Liberation*, 38.
15. Cone, *Black Theology of Liberation*, 81.

liberation for Black bodies under historic and everyday siege. Of the construct, Cone relays the following:

> In Black theology, Blacks are encouraged to revolt against the structures of white social and political power by affirming Blackness, but not because Blacks have a chance of "winning." What could the concept of "winning" possibly mean? Blacks do what they do because and only because they can do no other; and Black theology says simply that such action is in harmony with divine revelation.[16]

Cone strikes down the idea of a Black "win," which is ontologically, theoretically, and theologically much different from Black liberation in full, because the concept of the "win" is itself a transient and shifting position installed by whiteness to ensure that Black bodies never actualize any kind of material nor ontological freedom. Cone emphasizes that,

> the gospel offers no assurance of winning. Again, what could "winning" possibly mean? If it means what white racists mean by it—enslavement of human beings on the alleged basis of white supremacy—then, "God deliver us!" The idea of winning is a hang-up of liberal whites who want to be white and Christian at the same time; but they fail to realize that this approach is a contradiction in terms—Christianity and whiteness are opposites. Therefore, when whites say, "That approach will not win out," our reply must be: "What do you mean? Who's trying to win?"[17]

Cone's Black liberation theology articulates and maps the material conditions of possibility/actuality for Black bodies. Any type of "win," as articulated through gradualist, passive, and inevitably anti-Black (direct or internalized) lenses, is inert and not the goal of Black theology, which is a liberation *and* survival theology. Cone reminds that

16. Cone, *Black Theology of Liberation*, 18.
17. Cone, *Black Theology of Liberation*, 43.

> [t]he task of Black theology . . . is to analyze the nature of the gospel of Jesus Christ in the light of oppressed Blacks so they will see the gospel as inseparable from their humiliated condition, and as bestowing on them the necessary power to break the chains of oppression. This means that it is a theology of and for the Black community, seeking to interpret the religious dimensions of the forces of liberation in that community. . . . *The goal of Black theology is to interpret God's activity as related to the oppressed Black community.*[18]

Cone emphasizes that, under Black theology, the community is God, and an overturning of systems of whiteness and racial capitalism is in line with divine revelation. Cone offers that God is Black, and Black bodies are crafted in the image of God, with whom one becomes more closely aligned by overturning systems of whiteness that truncate and violate Black bodies. In order to achieve liberation and to access true revelation along theological lines, Black bodies must eschew white paradigms of being:

> In a world in which the oppressor defines right in terms of whiteness, humanity means an unqualified identification with Blackness. Black, therefore, is beautiful; oppressors have made it ugly. We glorify it because they despise it; we love it because they hate it. It is the Black way of saying, "To hell with your stinking white society and its middle-class ideas about the world. I will have no part in it."[19]

I argue that Cone extends an Afrofuturist lens through his theological pronouncement that affirms Blackness as beautiful. Blackness is *not* nonbeing or negation, but absolutely under siege and threat of being reduced to nonbeing: "Blacks live under sentence of death."[20] Following Cone's argument, in order to meet Black liberation, or to protract it in a way that reaches all Black bodies,

---

18. Cone, *Black Theology of Liberation*, 5 (emphasis added).

19. Cone, *Black Theology of Liberation*, 15.

20. Cone, *Black Theology of Liberation*, 11.

> [Black theology, which is survival theology] must speak with a passion consistent with the depths of the wounds of the oppressed. Theological language is passionate language, the language of commitment, because it is language which seeks to vindicate the afflicted and condemn the enforcers of evil. Christian theology cannot afford to be an abstract, dispassionate discourse on the nature of God in relation to humankind; such an analysis has no ethical implications for the contemporary forms of oppression in our society.[21]

Cone warns against making theological revelation, and theological paradigms overall, abstract:

> There is no "abstract" revelation, independent of human experiences, to which theologians can appeal for evidence of what they say about the gospel. God meets us in the human situation, not as an idea or concept that is self-evidently true. God encounters us in the human condition as the liberator of the poor and the weak, empowering them to fight for freedom because they were made for it. Revelation as the word of God, witnessed in scripture and defined by the creeds and dogmas of Western Christianity, is too limiting to serve as an adequate way of doing theology today. Theology . . . is the second step, a reflective action taken in response to the first act of a practical commitment in behalf of the poor.[22]

In essence, under Black theology, revelation is a tangible and material action that leads to a higher paradigm of self-knowing and self-affirming. Revelation leads to the pursuit of the elimination of all shackles of oppression in the world, and within that the annihilation of systems of anti-Blackness that delimit the movement, freedom, right to life, and quality of life of Black bodies on Earth. Black theology, as he writes, rejects theological imperatives held in hypothetical airs, or in eventuality, which are ultimately unconcerned with the immediate and permanent freeing of Black bodies. If God is Black, and divine revelation pushes us

21. Cone, *Black Theology of Liberation*, 17.
22. Cone, *Black Theology of Liberation*, xix.

to annihilate the shackles of domination that God himself once wore, and broke, Black theology mandates that Black liberation is a project that must continue *now,* on Earth. Cone writes that Black bodies encounter God on Earth through the recognition of their beauty and their chains, and that revelation pushes them to transform and transcend their condition, which inevitably means the destruction of whiteness by any means necessary.[23]

Overall, Cone indicts the internalization of white metrics of how Black bodies should be and move. He warns, "Black theology also rejects those who counsel Blacks to accept the limits which this society places on them, for it is tantamount to suicide. In existential philosophy suicide is the ultimate expression of despair. If we accept white definitions of Blackness, we destroy ourselves."[24]

I argue that white notions or definitions of Blackness are also commensurate with other anti-Black and white supremacist notions, such as heteronormativity, cissexism, trans-antagonism or transphobia, ableism, and so on. These -isms inhibit us from imagining—theologically, ontologically, and in terms of Afrofutures—the fullness of a Black body unencumbered by the chains that Cone commands us to remove once and for all.

In connection with Cone's indictment of white notions of being and of Blackness, I draw from Audre Lorde's concept of the *mythical norm* to describe the Eurocentric ideals of being that limit the conditions of possibility for the liberation of all Black bodies. Lorde's *mythical norm* is this:

> Somewhere, on the edge of consciousness, there is what [Lorde] call[s] a mythical norm, which each one of us within our hearts knows "that is not me." In America, this norm is usually defined as *white, thin, male, young, heterosexual, Christian, and financially secure.* It is with this mythical norm that the trappings of power reside within this society.[25]

---

23. Malcolm X, *By Any Means Necessary,* 35–67.
24. Malcolm X, *By Any Means Necessary,* 17.
25. Lorde, *Sister Outsider,* 116 (emphasis original).

While this mythic norm is a population Cone indicts, I find that placing Lorde in context with Cone helps to illuminate the dimensions of Blackness that are lost within normative considerations of Black bodies, which ultimately delays revelation that facilitates true and holistic Black liberation. I ask, what violence exists in the understanding of Black bodies as only normative? As exclusively able-bodied? As only heterosexual, and cisgender?

The 2017 statistics by the Human Rights Campaign and the Trans People of Color Coalition at this article's onset relay only a fraction of the sheer violence that exists at the hands of those who deem Black trans and queer bodies as errant. The quantitative data represents only the Black trans and queer bodies in the United States who were identified, and inevitably leaves out more who were misgendered in death by families, media outlets, and militarized police.

I extend Cone's work to interrogate and find more resonance with the Black theological—and within that, epistemological—concept of knowing that is cultivated through the process of revelation. Through others' work on queer theology, James Cone has aligned himself with queer bodies and has sought to make queer struggles visible given the resonance with anti-Black struggles, and the struggles of all oppressed people under racialized and gendered capitalism.

Paul Brandeis Raushenbush, Senior Vice President at Auburn Theological Seminary and editor of Auburn Seminary's online journal *Voices*, relays a critical and warm anecdote on what I would term as an intersectional[26] lens by James Cone. Raushenbush recalls:

> I remember my first theology paper which was an examination of the intersections of Black Theology and Queer Theology. Cone invited his students to understand how different communities understood God, especially communities that had lived under oppression. When Dr. Cone taught the section on LGBT history and theology, I could see how he relished quoting the profanity laden statements by the drag queens who stood up and refused to take the abuse anymore. Dr. Cone was generous that

26. Crenshaw, "Mapping the Margins."

way; he wanted people to know about the experience of oppression and terror that Black people had experienced in this country but he also was moved by other voices. He told me "God is a God that makes liberation meaningful to those who are marginalized no matter where they are. God takes on that identity of the oppressed."[27]

Cone's take on Black theology and Blackness is that Black theology is a theological, ontological, and epistemological mode of self-awareness and internal decolonization that allows one to galvanize towards total and unabashed revolution and liberation. Cone gave us a transformative understanding of the Bible itself: God is not simply being borrowed and arbitrarily Blackened; God is and always has been Black, and configurations of him that align more with whiteness are erroneous. Cone emphasizes that he is unconcerned with a Christian theology that is wholly abstract or distanced from the material conditions afflicting bodies on the ground. God is more closely identified with the "lacerations, woundings, fissures, . . . openings, ruptures, punctures of the flesh" that line Black bodies and reinterpret Black gender.[28] Any practitioner or worshipper must align themselves with racial justice and the dismemberment of systemic anti-Blackness if they truly, and adamantly, worship. To continue to allow systems of anti-Blackness to proliferate renders a body, and one's alleged status as a believer, inert. Cone raises that,

> if the oppressed of this land want to challenge the oppressive character of white society, they must begin by affirming their identity in terms of the reality that is antiwhite. Blackness, then, stands for all victims of oppression who realize that the survival of their humanity is bound up with liberation from whiteness.[29]

Cone's theology shows that Black theology can be a liberating force that is also transnational and intersectional. His life's work demonstrates an alignment with bodies maligned by the many evils

27. Raushenbush, "Dr. James Cone," para. 3.

28. Spillers, Hortense. "Mama's Baby, Papa's Maybe: An American Grammar Book." Baltimore: *Diacritics*, Summer 1987. p.67.

29. Cone, *Black Theology of Liberation*, 7.

of Eurocentricity and the violent project of whiteness, and of racialized-gendered capitalism. My work does not detect an obfuscation, but instead, a need to go further.

I concede to the differences in language that exist in the time in which Cone was writing, that exist in his 1986 revision, and from where I write today. I give credence to Cone's acknowledgment of Black feminism and womanism, and his critique of masculinist writings within Black philosophy and theology that ignore or create a present-absence about Black women. The language of trans, transgender, cisgender, many vibrant non-cisgenders, and the recent linguistic and semantic shift towards addressing systems of anti-trans violence as trans-antagonism is one that has largely been codified by younger trans bodies, though I contend that trans bodies, especially trans bodies of color, have always been articulating their oppression in words that are enough. Still, my work dives deeper into the specificities of transgender and Blackness, of Blackness-as-gender, in ways that Cone's intersectional analysis of revelation and Black liberation theology can situate.

Cone offers us a series of questions that search for the contours of Black liberation theology. In Part 1 of *A Black Theology of Liberation*, he says this:

> The Black experience forces us to ask, "What does revelation mean when one's being is engulfed in a system of white racism cloaking itself in pious moralities?" "What does God mean when a police officer whacks you over the head because you are Black?" "What does the church mean when white churchmen say they need more time to end racism?"[30]

Cone provides answers to his own ponderings by reminding that "Black theology is concerned only with the tradition of Christianity that is usable in the Black liberation struggle. As it looks over the past, it asks: 'How is the Christian tradition related to the oppression of Blacks in America?'"[31] He emphasizes that religion is

---

30. Cone, *Black Theology of Liberation*, 24.
31. Cone, *Black Theology of Liberation*, 25.

not "irrelevant altogether; . . . religion unrelated to Black liberation is irrelevant."[32]

For Cone, Black liberation theology is something not ensconced inside the physical walls of churches. The Black church does have an immense level of power and credence over Black theology. Cone writes,

> In the New Testament the church (*ecclesia*) is the community that has received the Holy Spirit and is now ready to do what is necessary to live out the gospel. It is the assembly of those who have become heirs of the promises of God; and because they have experienced what that means for humanity, they cannot accept the world as it is. They must rebel against evil so all citizens may know that they do not have to behave according to unjust societal laws.[33]

To be truly liberatory and arbitrators of a Black theology, the church must be committed to ending systemic and communal violence against all peoples. However, Black theology is itself an ontological and teleological paradigm that is representative of bodies who align themselves with the obliteration of all facets of white supremacy and Eurocentric hegemony. What does it mean, though, for the revelatory work of knowing and self-knowing to be held up within the Black church out of rejection of the fullness of Blackness, i.e. the relationship of Blackness to transness? Cone argues that "the contemporary Christ is in the Black ghetto, making decisions about white existence and Black liberation."[34] If the contemporary Christ is ultimately concerned with bodies most imbricated and dispossessed by axioms of power, especially *Black* bodies at increased axioms of power, could the contemporary Christ not be a Black trans poet, indicting other manifestations of anti-Black oppressions—anti-Black-trans and anti-Black queer violence—that go invisible to normative, or cis and heterosexual eyes?

For Cone, theology must always be a liberation theology, a bodied mode of meaning-making, and a passionate theology that

32. Cone, *Black Theology of Liberation*, 58, 59.

33. Cone, *Black Theology of Liberation*, 130.

34. Cone, *Black Theology of Liberation*, 39.

allows for and necessitates the survival of Black bodies, given the relationality of Blackness to non-cis or transgender due to the colonial fissures made on the Black body.[35] Cone's interrogation does not question the ability of Black bodies to liberate from the system of anti-Blackness. Rather, he merges an Afropessimist understanding of a world imbued in an anti-Black terrain with an Afrofuturist arraignment of what liberation could even mean, must contain, and how it can be protracted. Part of this liberation, or Black ontological and theological liberation requires epistemological understanding of Blackness itself:

> To know God is to know about ourselves, our beautiful Black selves. . . . It is a contemporary decision about a contemporary event, the event of Black and white beings. Revelation is a historical liberation of an oppressed people from slavery. When an oppressed people comes to know who it is, it will not tolerate oppression. This is the key to self-understanding.[36]

Cone also argues that Blackness necessitates a commitment to protracting liberation for all Black bodies, especially because, as Audre Lorde argues through the concept of the *mythic norm*, classism, colonialism, misogynoir,[37] transphobia/transantagonism, ableism, and so on, are bound up in anti-Blackness. Cone finds that,

> Black thinkers are in a different position. They cannot be Black and identified with the powers that be. To be Black is to be committed to destroying everything this country loves and adores. Creativity and passion are possible when one stands where the Black person stands, the one who has visions of the future because the present is unbearable. And the Black person will cling to that future as a means of passionately rejecting the present.[38]

In this detailing of what Black thought and Black theology must take up, Cone is also indicting Black churches that take up

35. Spillers, Hortense. "Mama's Baby, Papa's Maybe," 67.

36. Cone, *Black Theology of Liberation*, 54.

37. Bailey, "They Aren't Talking about Me. . ."

38. Cone, *Black Theology of Liberation*, 20.

the work of gradualism or reinscribe chains borrowed from white supremacist notions that constrict Black bodies. I extend his indictment to focus on Black bodies who allow for, as Alexander Weheliye terms, biopolitical racializing assemblages that disallow the fullness of Black expression, especially expression, embodiment, and knowledge that is Black, queer, and trans.[39] What does it mean, then, when Black bodies who abide by Black theological discourses exclusively abide by a project of liberation for bodies deemed and self-identifying as normative, or specifically for cis and heterosexual bodies? In this paper, I argue that the Black church is inhibited from true, honest, and legitimate Black liberation because of its failure to access revelation through the knowing and acknowledgment of Black trans and queer bodies. I argue that Black trans and queer folks are protracting and doing revelation through body work, which is revelation that the normative confines of the Black church ignores. My paper addresses not so much a teleological concern of whether revelation can happen, but whether normative Black bodies can catch up to the work that is being forged by Black trans and queer bodies.

Cone argues that religion must be codified along lines of Blackness and Black liberation; Christian theology must take shape as a method of theological expression for bodies under domination. He insists that:

> to be passionate, Black theology may find it necessary to break with traditional theological concerns. Such concerns are often unrelated to oppressed existence . . . it believes that racism is incompatible with the gospel of Christ, and it must, therefore, do everything it can to reveal the satanic nature of racism, so that it can be destroyed.[40]

I move to extend his indictment of the church's code of moral purity that has ousted calls towards the very insurgence upon which the Black Christian church is founded. My concern is that current, normative conceptualizations of Black liberation and Black

39. Weheliye, *Habeas Viscus*.
40. Weheliye, *Habeas Viscus*, 20.

liberation theology are illegitimate because they obfuscate these cata-
lytic bodies—Black trans and queer bodies—which are intrinsic to
the formation of Blackness. The Black church's break with immediate
insurgence and the internalization of a biopolitical moral code is evident when examining who, in fact, remains visible and present in the
archives of history. Cone speaks of this code, but does not fully articulate the queerness and transness that the Black Christian church
expressly disallows. An icon in his own right, Bayard Rustin was
eschewed and made illegible in the old Civil Rights Movement and
in Martin Luther King Jr.'s campaign solely for possessing a Blackness that was queer. As Imani Perry asserts in her 2018 text, *Looking
for Lorraine: The Radiant and Radical Life of Lorraine Hansberry*, we
are still searching for Lorraine Hansberry, a Black gay poet on many
of the frontlines of the Civil Rights Movement who wrote towards
a Black and liberated future in ways that, until recently, have been
obfuscated.[41] I contend that the discourses of Black liberation are imbued within heteronormative conceptualizations, ontologically and
in terms of material positioning. In other words, the liberation, the
act or embodiment of "overcoming" that is situated or extolled from
and by the Black Christian church, is situated within, as Cone argues, white—and as I extend, cis and heteronormative—conceptual
geographies, or grounds, that foreclose the multitudinous potential
of Black gender, and the intrinsicness of transness to Blackness. Cone
asserts that religion that moves away from or severs connection with
Black liberation is itself null and inert. Where might we find Rustin?
Hansberry? Most prominently, what does it mean for a Black liberation that is expressed in terms of, and expressly for, bodies who are cis
and/or heterosexual? What Black liberation through the Black Christian church is fungible or possible for Black trans and nonbinary
bodies? In what ways does a Black liberatory politic that obfuscates
or omits the intrinsicness of Black nonnormative genders to any con-
ceptualization of Black revelation and liberation fail to examine the
full potential of a Black liberation and the fruit that it bears—specifically, in the overturning of violent, rigid, and gendered prohibitions
surrounding the Black body?

41. Perry, *Looking for Lorraine*.

In this paper, I assert an inherent discursivity between Blackness and transness, and that Black gender inherently defies and exists far from the fringes of colonial binaries. I situate Black gender as the gender of Blackness—Blackness as the gender—with special attention to Black genders deemed nonnormative: Black women's genders, Black men's genders, and primarily, Black trans and queer genders, Black non-cisgenders, and agenders. Given the lack of attention to these obscured bodies, my project asserts an inherent dialectic or syncretism between Blackness, queerness, and transness as developed and articulated by C. Riley Snorton, Marquis Bey, and Zenaida Peterson.

I analyze how Snorton, Bey, and Peterson develop concepts surrounding Black gender. I examine how Snorton and Bey conduct trans readings of Achille Mbembe's theory of *necropolitics* as a critique of teleological and positivist democratic conceptualizations of the body[42] that disallow for bodies deemed abject to live within nation-states or in particular ontologies (Christian ontologies, for example).[43] Mbembe's *necropolitics* asserts that "to exercise sovereignty is to exercise control over mortality and to define life as the deployment and manifestation of power."[44] Mbembe's work extends to a teleological understanding that Black death under a biopolitical-necropolitical state is the fundamental means of securing life for the white West. Unfortunately, Mbembe is deeply cis-masculinist in his extensions of Foucauldian *biopolitics*—necropolitics—which contributes to the academic and social erasure of Black trans and queer bodies. Still, aware of Mbembe's obfuscation of Black trans bodies, Marquis Bey and C. Riley Snorton invert and expressly read *necropolitics* conducted by nation-states (and bodies in service of their violent teleological and democratic imperatives, i.e., death) as not only an anti-Black project, but inherently an anti-Black-trans project. *Necropolitics* as anti-Black-trans is knowledge that exists because of the inherent diffusiveness between transness

42. This language was largely shaped by a series of conversations with one of my research preceptors, Profé. Jared Rodríguez, a PhD candidate at the time of this article's drafting.

43. Mbembé and Meintjes, "Necropolitics," 11–40.

44. Mbembé and Meintjes, "Necropolitics," 12.

and Blackness, the distinct policing of Black gender, and the lived experiences of Black trans bodies under body policing by their respective nation-states. Black gender defies Eurocentric configurations of gender, and like Cone's articulation of the white liberal "win," Black bodies can never configure neatly into the reductive frame of man/woman, or the sexually dimorphic binary of male/female, a binary that inherently obfuscates intersex bodies. Many of us Black trans and queer bodies recognize this and ultimately do not seek to configure into these colonial and transgressive binaries.

I press for a Black theopolitical and christological configuration that encompasses the totality of all Black bodies. In M. Shawn Copeland's text *Enfleshing Freedom,* she asks, "Can a Christology incorporate all dimensions of corporality?"[45] I follow Copeland's line of inquiry by examining the dimensions of resistance possible for all Black bodies under Christology. The stakes of this configuration are high. The Black church has been the site of Black organizing for the old Civil Rights Movement and is the site in which many Black bodies are reared. There also exist deep roots of violence of the Black church in the American South. The complex and reductive renderings of gender, Blackness, and ultimately Black gender within Black Christian theological discourses discredit the fullness of Blackness, and are complicit in the adamant and inherently vile denial of Black trans bodies. Reductive renderings of Black gender limit the conditions of possibility for a Black liberation that might be housed in part in the Black church. What would it mean for Black children, forced to be in proximity to theological discourses, to understand that their genders, however they might take shape, are not abject? What would it mean for the Black church to foster revelation in that way? What would it mean for there to be a holistic expansion of what truly becomes possible with Black liberation through the reworking of gender understood by the Black church, which has centered itself as a site of refuge, but for bodies deemed normative?

Again, Cone emphasizes that: "In [Black bodies] God becomes oppressed humanity and thus reveals that the achievement of full humanity is consistent with divine being. Blackness is a

45. Copeland, *Enfleshing Freedom,* 78.

manifestation of the being of God in that it reveals that neither divinity nor humanity reside in white definitions but in liberation from captivity."[46]

Given the epistemic violence that resides in the Black church's understandings of Black bodies, and violent obfuscations of Black trans and queer folks, can there be true revelation and alignment with Blackness within and by the Black church? If humans do theology, what are the stakes of a Black theology that writes Black transness out of theological and liberatory paradigms? In Cone's venerable tradition, I interrogate the conditions of possibility for Black trans and queer bodies under Black theological discourses. Using his language and light, what becomes visible when we mine for conditions of legibility for Black trans and queer people? Can the Black church truly protract Black liberation without an acknowledgment of the transformative body work that Black trans and queer folks are doing?

In the hallowed halls of my family church, I must sign the visitor's book. The stained-glass windows are inscribed with hymns that have been tucked into my chest. I must know that the presence of the Lord is one ephemeral, here-and-gone, circumstantial, but allegedly alienated by my queerness inextricable; attracted only by a distinct lineage that does not possess all of my kin.

The perennial struggle for civil rights and Black liberation was originally able to take root in Black churches of myriad Christian denominations because of the theology's premise: salvation, liberation, and a new temporality for the abused on Earth. Black bodies under constant siege took refuge behind stained-glass windows with texts that promised recovery. In the deepest niches of the Jim Crow South, my great-grandmother sought a family church that would bear her lineage. There, she demanded her favorite hymnal be sung there during her last Sunday on Earth. Her daughter has buried two mothers, two husbands, and one son, all taken by the same plague: cancers caught too late, and too little money for finer care; overwork; depression, PTSD, and anxiety undetected and

---

46. Cone, *Black Theology of Liberation*, 121.

silenced. The crucifix of the Jim Crow South, of anti-Blackness, underscores the recorded cause of death.

Liberation is by no means here. If anything, the line of Black women in the front pews, showing how the artillery of whiteness has weathered their skins, asserts that point by virtue of their existences.

Yet, still, I make room for minor concessions: though the fact of liberation is not one that has been fully actualized, what does it mean for the Black church, specifically Black cis, nonqueer bodies, to believe that they possess the makings of Black liberation without Black trans and queer bodies?

A GENDER IN FLUX: BLACK TRANS BODIES AND BLACK LIBERATORY DISCOURSES

In any consideration of Black liberation, there must be an expansion, or a recognition of the expanded nature, of Black gender that defies male/female dimorphism. In "Mama's Baby, Papa's Maybe," Hortense Spillers articulates that the inherent mutability of gender/s of/on Black bodies is the direct result of the colonial project of the trans-Atlantic slave trade that created violent fissures on our captive bodies, fissures that we reopened by the workings of neoliberal and necropolitical nation-states. In *Black on Both Sides: A Racial History of Trans Identity,* published in 2017, C. Riley Snorton draws from Spillers to produce a raced historiography of trans identity that understands Black gender as mutable, in part due to the slavery-industrial complex. Snorton quotes Spillers on a later section of "Mama's Baby, Papa's Maybe":

> [T]he female, in this order of things, breaks in upon the imagination with a forcefulness that marks both a denial and an "illegitimacy." Because of this peculiar American denial, the Black American male embodies the only American community of males which has had the specific occasion to learn who the female is within itself, the infant child who bears the life against the could-be fateful gamble, against the odds of pulverization and murder, including her own. It is the heritage of the mother that

the African-American male must regain as an aspect of
his own personhood—the power of "yes" to the "female"
within.[47]

In order to reckon with the fissures created on captive flesh
by colonial violence, Spillers argues that African-American men
imbued in contexts of cishypermasculinity and misogynoir must
accept and say "yes" to the Black femininity that is invested within
their bodies. Spillers's argument indicts what we would today,
through the work of Moya Bailey, term as misogynoir, a term with
which Spillers's work resonates, and anti-Blackness within the 1968
Moynihan report that her article takes up. The Moynihan report,
written by a white man, regards the makeup of Black familial structures as unstable or errant[48] and masculinizes to degenders Black
women in order to emasculate Black men. At the threat of emas-
culation, Black men reflect the ideas of the report by moving to
become hypermasculine at the expense of Black women's bodies,
which is another extension of misogynoir. Spillers makes room to
analyze how the misogynoir that is marketed by Black men—and,
I'd argue, specifically cisgender and heterosexual Black men—is
itself a kind of internalization that ignores the linage of the/a Black
Mother that is constitutive to his being. Spillers speaks of a holistic
reinscription of Black gender from the hegemonic fringes of cis,
colonialist male/female binaries: "This body whose flesh carries the
female and the male to the frontiers of survival bears in person the
marks of a cultural text whose inside has been turned outside."[49]
Black bodies carry, blur, and make indistinguishable or mutable the
biopolitical/necropolitical bounds of how bodies can thus appear.
Blackness, as Spillers and Snorton argue, has a mutable gender due
to the project of chattel slavery and necropolitical violence, like the
1968 Moynihan report, which ignores racial capitalism and refers
to Black bodies as abject for not siloing themselves into white configurations of gender. Black bodies, and I argue especially Black

47. Spillers, "Mama's Baby, Papa's Maybe," 80.
48. Spillers, "Mama's Baby, Papa's Maybe," 74.
49. Spillers, "Mama's Baby, Papa's Maybe," 67.

trans and queer bodies, are conducting the vulnerable project of mimesis against this colonial hegemonic grammar.

Importantly, then, C. Riley Snorton and Marquis Bey perform a necessary intervention to illuminate the historic and natural existence of Black trans and queer bodies, in a way that contests the lethal and historic tradition of pathologizing Black bodies. They note that Black trans and queer bodies arise out of precolonial contexts—or, before hegemonic and Eurocentric orderings of bodies into white men and white women's genders—inasmuch as they arise in direct opposition to the demands of a neocolonial and necropolitical ordering of life. They trans/queer the work of Achille Mbembe's *necropolitics* by identifying a deep and inextricable connection between Blackness and transness—to invoke Bey's terminology, the Blackness of transness; the transness of Blackness.[50] Together, Blackness and transness are all the more endemically persecuted by the wealthy and powerful nation-state, and their mandates on identity formation and visibility. Says Bey of Black trans (in)visibility in public arenas in his article "The Trans*ness of Blackness, the Blackness of Trans*ness":

> The necropolitical and carceral state govern the politics of public space, which is a space predicated upon the assumption of the impossibility of Blackness, transness, and Black transness: a hegemonic grammar that utterly disallows the very possibility of transgender; . . . This could also be said to be the case with Black bodies occupying space implicitly coded in and through whiteness.[51]

Asserting a discursiveness and diffusiveness between Black bodies and trans bodies does not code or engender all trans bodies as Black, and vice versa—rather, a reading of this discursiveness recognizes the relationality of disparate bodies spaced into disparate categorizations. There *is no* Blackness without a recognition of the dynamism that inherently resides within it, and without recognition of the way that Black bodies do gender differently. Black theologian M. Jacqui Alexander provides a lens of seeing Black

---

50. Bey, "Trans*-Ness of Blackness, the Blackness of Trans*-Ness," 277.

51. Bey, "Trans*-Ness of Blackness, the Blackness of Trans*-Ness," 277.

trans bodies, in the context of Cone's Black theology of liberation, as bodies already committed to self-knowing and self-venerating as the task of liberatory revelation commands. What becomes visible when we understand Black trans bodies as inherently connected to the transformative theological paradigm of revelation to its fullest potential? Can we see Black trans bodies as always-already committed to the very paradigms that Black theology commands of Black trans bodies? Can we understand Black theological revelation as insufficient without an understanding and legitimate acknowledgment of Black trans bodies as intrinsic and ineffaceable from Blackness?

In her 2006 text *Pedagogies of Crossing: Meditations on Feminism, Sexual Politics, Memory, and the Sacred*, M. Jacqui Alexander utilizes African cosmologies and Christology to articulate an anti-imperial body politic that reformats theses of salvation and liberation. She blends a consideration of Black queerness (and, I read, transness) with her analysis of Black Christology. I borrow her articulation of the palimpsest, which is "a parchment that has been inscribed two or three times, the previous text having been imperfectly erased and remaining therefore still partly visible."[52] She contends that this "imperfect erasure, hence visibility, of a 'past'"[53] is especially palpable in the context of bodies under domination and on demonic grounds, to invoke the language of Katherine McKittrick and Sylvia Wynter, wherein the suffering and violation of colonized bodies in their disparate locations is altogether imbricated and layered. I argue that Black trans bodies exist as testaments to the ancestral project, lineage, and heritage of gender imbued with Blackness, or Black gender. Black trans bodies are palimpsests for liberation. Black trans bodies exist because of the gendering and ungendering in which Black bodies are bound, but also because of the palimpsest of Black gender that defies, and always has resisted, colonial gender markers. Black trans bodies are not to be understood as tragic, but rather as resilient, beautiful, and *real* products

---

52. Alexander, *Pedagogies of Crossing*, 190.
53. Alexander, *Pedagogies of Crossing*, 190.

of the immemorial uniqueness of Blackness and the ungendering of Black bodies.

I argue that Black trans poet Zenaida Peterson's body exemplifies this palimpsest, and the mutability of gender due to slavery, systems of anti-Blackness, and out of both survival and love by Black trans bodies. In the tradition of Spillers and Snorton, Black trans poet Zenaida Peterson inscribes the notion of Black gender as mutable in a new, succinct grammar through spoken word. In their poem "My Pronouns are Black," Zenaida Peterson interrogates this relationality of Blackness and transness, or the mutability of Black gender against the hegemonic constructions of gender that have been forced onto their body: "How do you go from a slave to a gendered thing/from a mule to a person/and expect gender to function the same across race?"[54] Peterson performs a necessary, and rhetorical, inquiry directed at Black bodies who only accept or acknowledge normative, or cis and heterosexual Black bodies. Black trans and queer bodies are most importantly and inalienably committed to disrupting and destroying gender that disallows the mutability of gender on Black bodies, or Black gender itself. Cone articulates that Black theology "represents that community of Blacks who refuse to cooperate in the exaltation of whiteness and the degradation of Blackness. It proclaims the reality of the biblical God who is actively destroying everything that is against the manifestation of Black human dignity."[55] I extend that Black trans and queer bodies are some of the only bodies committed to this total obliteration of the confines of Eurocentric, sexual-dimorphic gender configurations that impede true Black liberation, and beyond that, an honest theology that is committed to the destruction of all structures of power.

Normative considerations of the Black body require a singularity of spirit, in direct contrast to Black and indigenous genders that allow for a multiplicity of soul.[56] What would it mean to understand

54. Peterson, "'My Pronouns Are Black,'" 1:31–1:40.

55. Cone, *Black Theology of Liberation*, 55–56.

56. Enos, Tony. "8 Things You Should Know." Tony Enos describes an indigenous gender, two-spirit, wherein bodies possess two spirits, or both the man and woman genders within their bodies. The gender is expressly non-cis and

the impossibility of separating the body and the soul, as colonialism demands and as Black transness rejects? To understand physical elements, like the Eucharist or communion, as body work that follows the lineage of body work and self-knowing that Black trans and queer bodies produce? What would it mean, in tandem, to transition spirituality out of the physical space of the church to our bodies, as Black transness so cosmically does? Black trans writers Zenaida Peterson and Hari Ziyad offer us "a language in which to dwell,"[57] or a language that offers up the revelatory and liberatory work that Black trans and queer bodies are already protracting. They lay out the ways in which normative Black bodies, and I extend, the Black church, eschew epistemological ways of knowing Blackness through the abjection of non-cis and nonqueer Black bodies. In Peterson's dynamic poem "My Pronouns are Black," and in Ziyad's 2017 AFROPUNK article "My Gender Is Black," they offer the foundation upon which we might carve out space for Black trans bodies in Black christological discourses—or rather, eliminate the spaces that do not offer room for our bodies.

"YOU TAUGHT ME THAT": TRANS-ANCESTRAL INTERVENTIONS ON THE GENDERS OF THE BLACK BODY

Black non-cis poet, writer, and organizer Hari Ziyad articulates as a politic of ancestral knowledge as complicit in ontological meaning-making that forms. Ziyad will here be referred to using they/them pronouns and their last name. Ziyad takes up Spillers's work in their 2017 AFROPUNK article, "My Gender Is Black," in order to articulate a Black trans historiography that detects and emphasizes the mutability of Black gender. They indict white and colonial formations of gender that are inherently foreclosed to the breadth, beauty, and generative nature of Blackness. Blackness alone creates space for myriad conditions of possibility for gender, ontology, and movement that has always existed outside of the Euro-Western

defies colonial gender markers.

57. Morrison, "James Baldwin," para. 3.

terrain of limited, and essentialist dimorphic sex/gender formations. The article begins with Ziyad overhearing an interrogation
spoken by a Black child on their gender and relationship with their
partner, spoken to their Black woman mother—"Why can't they be
normal boys?"[58] In the article, the mother brushes off the question,
but looks at Hari in dismissal of their body:

> Initially, I turned to whom I assumed to be his mother
> expecting her to chastise him for the outburst, but she
> just stared at me as well with a slight grimace on her face.
> "Yes," she said without saying, "why can't you be a nor-
> mal boy?" *He had to learn it from somewhere,* I realized.
> But where did she? And where did I learn what I know
> about my gender? And what do I know?[59]

The dialogue against Ziyad here is similar to the interrogation posed by the white child to a Black man in Fanon's "The Fact
of Blackness." In Frantz Fanon's *Black Skins, White Masks,* a white
French child illustrates the infantile processes of colonialism by
forcing a Black man's body into a third consciousness, calling to him
in violent jest on the streets at his mother's side: "Look, a Negro!"[60]
The contours of the white French child's interrogation of the Black
man's body are in parallel to the violent tropes that enforce the pas-
sivity and dehumanization of Black women, to misreadings and ex-
ploitations of the biblical chapter of Leviticus, to the misgendering
in violent death of Black trans bodies, and is surmised in the interrogation and inquisition of the Black child wrapped up in the complex and violent lattices of cis- and heteronormativity—"Why can't
[Hari] be a normal boy?"[61] The theological and linguistic attempts
at unraveling and reclaiming bodies who are held up to impossible
colonial metrics are fraught, and difficult. Still, the thunders of the
Civil Rights Movement mantra by Black men, "I am a Man," and
Sojourner Truth's "Ain't I a Woman?" echo in direct response to an
anti-Blackness that kills.

58. Ziyad, "My Gender Is Black," para. 1.
59. Ziyad, "My Gender Is Black," para. 2 (emphasis original).
60. Fanon, *Black Skins, White Masks,* 112.
61. Ziyad, "My Gender Is Black," para. 2.

In response to the violent inquisition Ziyad writes: "No matter how much I explained, the world never seemed to make enough room for my being. I am only now realizing that this is because Blackness ruptures the laws of gender just like the laws of the state seem intent on rupturing Black life. My gender is Black."[62]

To return to "Mama's Baby, Papa's Maybe," Spillers situates Black gender at the nexus of constantly being regarded as illegitimate, errant, and inhuman.[63] The compliment to this assertion might be Fanon's "straddling Nothingness and Infinity," where he describes the endless and impossible stratification of his Black body across lines of ontology/possibility.[64] This straddling, ontological acrobatics, makes Fanon weep, though in the book's introduction he also describes that impossible space as an "extraordinarily sterile and arid region, an utterly naked declivity where an authentic upheaval can be born."[65] Ziyad, to extend on Fanon's assertion, regards Black gender as unable to be indexed by European spheres of what is deemed normative:

> Black people are out of step with womanhood and manhood. Black gender is always gender done wrong, done dysfunctionally, done in a way that is not "normal."
> . . . But instead of accepting the impossibility of Black gender as reality, and using it to create a different, freer, understandings of Black being, we are pressured to force our way into categories that weren't just not made for us, but *designed specifically for our exclusion.*[66]

Ziyad's gender is not blank, not an absence, but Black.[67] Ziyad's gender is also breaking out of the violent webs of white gender formation, which is a colonial binary that is predicated on the obfuscation and obliteration of Black trans bodies. Those same binaries can never fully encapsulate moves, mimesis, presentation,

62. Ziyad, "My Gender Is Black," para. 6.

63. Spillers, "Mama's Baby, Papa's Maybe," 74.

64. Fanon, *Black Skins, White Masks,* 10.

65. Fanon, *Black Skins, White Masks,* 10.

66. Ziyad, "My Gender Is Black," para. 10 (emphasis original).

67. Philip, *Black.*

and ontology of a Black body that is always in (ontological, physical, social, political, etc.) transition. The parroting of these normative confines and the adamant rejection of Black gender might be, I argue, tantamount to Cone's mandate of dismantling structures of whiteness: "Black theology represents that community of Blacks who refuse to cooperate in the exaltation of whiteness and the degradation of Blackness."[68] To be invested in structures of whiteness, or white gender formations that are expressly anti-Black-trans, is to be against the work of Black theology, which cannot exist divorced from Black gender formations, and pushing for the liberation of Black trans and queer bodies, of all Black bodies from garroting by European gender construction. Can the Black church truly articulate Black theology when it does not practice the epistemes of self-knowing that the Black body has so diligently cultivated? I don't feel that legitimate revelation can occur without those intimate and radical ways of knowing and seeing.

Zenaida Peterson (they/them pronouns) scalds the white infrastructures of gender, parroted from Black bodies who deem themselves normative to Black bodies who live in the ancestral genders that Blackness owned before and during the occupations of our bodies; and who live in the geography of absence—or, rather, abundance—uncharted by binary body configurations. Peterson is a Black trans poet and organizer from Boston, who writes on their Black trans and queer life in ways that interrupt the violences that riddle their body.

In "My Pronouns Are Black," which happened to be digitally released on the Youtube channel *SlamFind* in the same summer that Ziyad released their *AFROPUNK* article "My Gender Is Black," Peterson begins and ends with a tracing of their mother. Peterson inaugurates their work with, "I woke up to my mama's voice and it wasn't erasure./Sometimes I wake up a boy, switch to nothing by noon, go to sleep a girl./My pronouns are Black. My pronouns code-switch."[69] Peterson closes out the piece with,

---

68. Cone, *Black Theology of Liberation*, 55.
69. Peterson, "'My Pronouns Are Black,'" 0:03–0:21.

> My gender starts every poem about my mama, who
> don't wanna hear about the things white people taught
> me anymore. I say, white people didn't teach me how to
> be brown, how to overcome, how to gender. Mama, my
> body taught me that. Our ancestors taught me that. You
> taught me that. I watched you.[70]

Resoundingly, Peterson shouts that wrong is not their name.[71] The ancestral interventions on gender, if unacknowledged, are evident; Peterson illuminates how, similar to Spillers's intervention, all Black bodies are cultivating Black gender in disparate ways due to chattel-slavery and the immemorial modes of Black, Afro-ascended gender itself. In Peterson's work, gender on the Black body functions as something malleable. Black gender is something that is predicated on survival in the belly of an anti-Black, and expressly anti-transgression of Eurocentric gender binaries, world—"My pronouns are silent; are polite with strangers. My pronouns avoid the police./*The Black of me wants to survive long enough to have an identity politic.*"[72] Gender on Black bodies functions in the way it does because it is positioned on Black bodies that were never meant to own their bodies, let alone manifest or reinterpret or constantly queer/trans/Blacken how gender can look. Black bodies control and reinterpret (in)visibility.

Peterson writes that their pronouns "understand the significance of the Mason-Dixon in a Southern summertime—they are the Belle, the Peach, the 'yes, ma'am' they need to be and it does not render them invisible the way it is supposed to."[73] This navigation is itself an ontology and praxis of survival. To complement, Spillers's "Mama's Baby, Papa's Maybe" traces the lineage of Black women's bodies, and the ways that they have been both sliced physically and ontologically in service of chattel-slavery and necropolitical state initiatives. Black women's bodies have, as a result, inherited a plurality of labors and grotesque minimizations that are intended to

---

70. Peterson, "'My Pronouns Are Black,'" 2:18–2:42.

71. Jordan, "Poem about My Rights."

72. Peterson, "'My Pronouns Are Black,'" 1:02–1:14 (italics mine).

73. Peterson, "'My Pronouns Are Black,'" 1:45–1:54.

masculinize as a means of dehumanizing. In their poem, Peterson writes that "[their] pronouns see [their] mama play every gender role."[74] Peterson makes visible Spillers's theoretical parsing of Black bodies, and Spillers's work is but the ancestral buttress to Peterson's digitized indictment on the denial of Black gender by everyone, but in especially painful ways by Black bodies who deem themselves not-abject and normative in spite of how they do gender in similar ways to similar ends—survival, joy, and liberation.

Peterson is offering a resounding roadmap of the ways in which their gender manifests, contorts, and changes, and how it is absolutely inextricable from Black modes of fugitivity, meaning-making, and religiosity. For Peterson, their pronouns in the way that they use them are not simply a complementary negation of whiteness, but exist in Blackness given the ways that they act in service of Peterson's body, and how they are inherently imbued with the life and meaning-making produced by Peterson's Black body. Given the violations imposed upon Black bodies, Peterson has dreamed up a polemic that affirms that Black trans bodies have always existed before and will always exist beyond the limiting contours of Eurocentric gender binaries that position bodies along dimorphic lines to make such bodies more accessible, in order to make them more reducible. Peterson's work affirms that a revelation is needed by Black non-trans bodies that tout themselves as normative *because* Black gender is orchestrated in such a way that requires beautiful unfixity, fugitivity, and mimesis. Black non-cis bodies are simply open about the ways in which that ontological movement occurs. Peterson makes visible the multiplicity of gender within Blackness that is as much intrinsic to Blackness as it is ancestral. Blackness reveals itself as a gender for Black bodies given the legacy of fugitivity, transition, and breadth that exceeds the limitations of white gender binaries. Gender as Black, or the Blackness of gender, is forged out of Black trans and queer technologies of survival. Peterson navigates the world in a way that necessitates both fugitive transformation and resurfacing of ancestral ties to Black gender.

74. Peterson, "'My Pronouns Are Black,'" 0:35–0:38.

Peterson's mediations on movement and being, mediations that seem to rest at the very core of Blackness itself, are active, and can be categorized as a kind of body work in protraction of freedom. Peterson joins Black theologian M. Shawn Copeland in describing bodies as directly invested in the cosmological and theological work of protracting freedom. In *Enfleshing Freedom*, M. Shawn Copeland inscribes the Eucharist, or communion, as body work that, at its core, is positioned to transform bodies or galvanize them towards salvation.[75] What is the Eucharist but body work? Similarly, what is Peterson's body of work and body's work but an act of transformation and a continual spiritual practice? Peterson allows us their body as a lens through which we might see, and accept, the integrity of Blackness as trans, and of transness as Black; as a medium that displays Black gender as the palimpsest of Blackness. Their poem mandates a teleological reconfiguration of Blackness as intrinsically trans. If, for Cone, Black theology is survival theology, we might also understand Peterson's Black transgender and trans-ancestral mediations on being, body, gender, and movement, and towards freedom, security, and liberation of their Black trans body, as survival theology at work, or a central component of Black theology in its own right.[76] Peterson exalts themselves towards not only survival, but liberation in full:

> I know how to survive myself./My gender is my mama and every other Black woman calling me "girl."/My gender sees themself in the callouses of people who call me lovely./My gender loves my body so much; it sticks to me under all these clothes./In-between my legs, there is a nonbinary brown love letter written to the multitudes of me.[77]

I argue that Peterson's body of work *and* body work is a necessary contribution and intervention on Black theology, and that, Black trans reconfigurations and resignifications of the body are practices of the self-knowing and self-veneration that Cone

---

75. Copeland, *Enfleshing Freedom*.

76. Cone, *Black Theology of Liberation*, 17.

77. Peterson, "'My Pronouns Are Black,'" 1:54–2:18.

inscribes as part of liberatory theological revelation. Across the poem's lines, Peterson charts their body's movement across volatile public spaces, limiting home spaces that seek to disrupt their Black gender, and the interstices and fissures in which they find themselves most visible, and mine for a gender that is constantly in flux. I argue that Peterson reinscribes Black liberation theology to understand Black trans bodies as intrinsic to the formation of Blackness. They illuminate Black trans bodies as arbiters of a Black liberation theology that truly understands the urgency surrounding resignification of the flesh that acknowledges the unfixity and multitudinous potential of Black gender. This understanding of urgency is expressly related to an understanding of the totality of Blackness itself, and is expressly related to Cone's interpretation of revelation: "To know God is to know about ourselves, our beautiful Black selves. This is what revelation means to Blacks. It is a contemporary decision about a contemporary event, the event of Black and white beings."[78]

If revelation is about unveiling, is about the process that unveils knowledge about the Black body, or if the uncovering of true and intimate knowledge about Black bodies by Black bodies is inherently revelatory, I argue that there must be an understanding of the relationality of Blackness to transness given Black fugitivity and the ontological legacy of Black bodies negotiating selfhood along lines of flesh and gender. We might interpret Peterson's resounding call to their mother as both an indictment as well as an illumination—"You taught me that"[79]—of the ancestral knowledge that is both known and aged, and informs the gender and body of Peterson. In a December 2000 guest editorial in *Theological Studies*, M. Shawn Copeland indicts the intellectual obfuscation of Black theology by white Catholic theologians: "When will White Catholic theologians acknowledge the insights of Black theology as a permanently valid theological achievement? What other name can one give to this refusal and exclusion of Black insights but scotosis?"[80] I

78. Cone, *Black Theology of Liberation*, 54.
79. Peterson, "'My Pronouns Are Black,'" 2:36–2:39.
80. Copeland, "December 2000 editorial," para. 7.

borrow her use of the term *scotosis*, or intentional intellectual and social obfuscation, to conceptualize the Black Christology's refusal to detect the legibility of Black gender in its discourses on liberation. *Scotosis* might be understood as metonymy for the palimpsest as I employ it: it is upon the present-absence of Black gender that heteronormative Black Christology founds its liberation ideology.

Zenaida Peterson's haunting resound and call to their mother, "You taught me that,"[81] is an objection against the scotosis being conducted upon their body by their mother. Their body is the palimpsest, containing knowledge that undergirds the body even throughout its continual process of radical, Black, and trans resignification by Peterson. Hari Ziyad also does visibility work through the affirmation that their gender is Black, which is a powerful teleological indictment of an anti-Black-trans reduction of their bodies to colonial formations of gender. These indictments are expressly configured for bodies that believe a neat configuration of all gender; and specifically for white bodies who have never made the ontological journey through a dissecting enterprise predicated on servitude and dehumanization.

If the Black church is unwilling to assist in this process of resignification of the Black body, is a Black theology even at play?

CONCLUSION

There are no hymns that sing of me, or mine. There are no tongues in which our bodies, trans bodies, can be spoken. My intercession on Cone's work lies largely in an expansion of the terms of revelation, and a reinscription of a Black liberation theology that emphasizes the intrinsicness of Black gender to any formation of Blackness. I question if the Black church can even articulate a Black theology that is conducive to legitimate Black liberation for all Black bodies, or liberation that does not reinscribe anti-Black-trans and anti-Black-queer violence on Black trans and queer bodies—which is not liberation at all.

---

81. Peterson, "'My Pronouns Are Black,'" 2:36–2:39.

Cone argues that Black bodies should not altogether eschew theology simply because it has been tainted by whiteness, but that we must instead cultivate a Black theology of liberation that obliterates all structures of whiteness. He writes,

> Black theology cannot reject the future reality of life after death—grounded in Christ's resurrection—simply because whites have distorted it for their own selfish purposes. That would be like the Black Arts Movement, rejecting art because white artists have misused it. What is needed is redefinition in the light of the liberation of the black community.[82]

Cone emphasizes that Black theology is the legitimate theology, and the white theology is itself a distortion: "To receive God's revelation is to become Black with God by joining God in the work of liberation."[83]

Along the trajectory mapped by Peterson and Ziyad, I argue that there must be a dialogic and paradigmatic shift from hegemonic renderings of Black gender articulated by Black bodies deemed normative within Black theology. Peterson and Ziyad emphasize that the movements and motivations behind their bodies are inherently survival theologies, given the transformative and spiritual body work that they perform and embody towards their freedom and maintenance of life. Peterson and Ziyad extend Cone's articulation that resistance against all forms of violence and systemic oppression is a spiritual mandate for bodies under Black theological paradigms. It would be an oversimplification and generalization of their works to truncate the languages that they offer us as *only* simple calls to undo systems of anti-Black-trans violence.

This work is indeed absolutely crucial, but Peterson and Ziyad emphasize a necessary understanding of gender as Black, and Blackness as constituting a gender, as never outside of any contours of possibility nor actuality, and Black trans bodies as inherently connected to any utterance of a Black theology of survival and liberation. True Black revelation rests in a resignification of the flesh

---

82. Cone, *Black Theology of Liberation,* 141.

83. Cone, *Black Theology of Liberation,* 66.

(to return to Spillers) to truly understand the flux and the spiritual and ontological moves that all Black bodies endure as a result of gender and body work across generational lines, and as a result of the ontological gymnastics that Black bodies must perform in order to live.

Placing Peterson and Ziyad in context with departed ancestor Cone makes visible the need for a radical reinterpretation of Black gender, and the mandates of survival theology that must state the power of "yes"[84] to the multitudinous potential and actuality of Blackness within in order to articulate a Black body that *lives* in order to seek a survival theology, and as Peterson writes, "long enough to have an identity politic."[85] I argue that the survival theologies of Black trans bodies exist as ontological predecessors to heteronormative liberation theologies. In order for Black theology to position itself as a truly generative site of liberation, there must be an arraignment that situates Black trans life as the fulcrum of Blackness and any survival theology that dwells within it. There must be a reunification of the body to the soul under Black christological paradigms, a union that Black transness offers by virtue of its very being. The body work of Black trans poets, eulogizers, organizers, *bodies,* must be understood as expressly spiritual and transformative, and belonging to the archive of Black theology as much as cis and heterosexual preachers and writers have been situated.

But, can the Black church do or assist in this work of resignification?

I interrogate the conditions of possibility that unveil themselves when normative Black bodies interpret the physical, ontological, and epistemological movement of Black trans bodies as the roadmap for a Black survival theology towards liberation and freedom. I ask if a Black liberation politic and theology can include a veneration of the body in the way that Black trans bodies have learned to venerate ourselves. But is this truly possible or at the least, actionable?

---

84. Spillers, "Mama's Baby, Papa's Maybe," 80.
85. Peterson, "'My Pronouns Are Black,'" 1:11–1:14.

James Cone asks us to hold onto the future, and to understand the work of Black theology as interpreting and molding the future. In *A Black Theology of Liberation*'s discussion of eschatology, he writes: "This is precisely the meaning of our Lord's resurrection, and why we can fight against overwhelming odds. We believe in the future of God, a future that must become present."[86]

He continues:

> The future is still the future. This means that Black theology rejects elaborate speculations about the end. It is just this kind of speculation that led Blacks to stake their whole existence on heaven . . . Too much of this talk is not good for the revolution. Black theology believes that the future is God's future, as are the past and present. Our past knowledge and present encounter with God ground our confidence that the future will be both like and unlike the present—like the present in the encounter with God, and unlike it in the fullness of liberation as a reality.[87]

For Cone, the past is prologue, to echo the language of Julie Dash, and remains visceral and present as Black bodies articulate a future free of chains.[88] Cone moves to unmoor Black liberation from the chains of a white and Eurocentric eventuality that seats Black bodies in perpetual eventuality. I argue that a lack of acknowledgment of Black trans and queer bodies, and plain understanding of the mutability and malleability of Black gender, inhibits the Black church from inciting true revolution and Black liberation. Commensurately, without an understanding of Black trans bodies and Blackness as gender, any articulation of Black liberation actively recreates fissures, to draw from Spillers, that bind Black bodies to white notions of gender.

The hope that Cone inspires his readers to feel is towards an Afrofuture wherein Black bodies, and all oppressed bodies on Earth, are free. Actively working towards this freedom is an act of divine revelation; God is Black, Black bodies are God. Moving

---

86. Cone, *Black Theology of Liberation*, 141.

87. Cone, *Black Theology of Liberation*, 141.

88. Carter, "'What's Past is Prologue.'"

towards freedom is in alignment with unlocking divinity for bodies on Earth. I'd argue that, through their works that articulate the complex epistemes of self-knowing and self-affirmation, Zenaida Peterson and Hari Ziyad are already passionate Black theological bodies. But can the Black church meet them where they are? Is it too late? Can this radical paradigm shift that Black trans and queer bodies articulate be actualized by normative bodies in the Black church that have never wanted to deal with Black gender that doesn't configure itself with ease?

James Cone writes that the church, including the Black church, "must rebel against evil so all citizens may know that they do not have to behave according to unjust societal laws."[89] I ask, how committed is the Black church to dispelling the evils that are articulated inside of their own walls?

Perhaps my questions are leading—I should be more transparent. Cone's hope and faith in Black theology, and in a radical reworking of the Black church in order to move away from white gradualism into immediate work towards Black liberation, is warming. It is a condition of possibility, which he might have seen as an actuality, that I want. To have the Black church understand Black genders, from infancy onwards, understood as in harmony with divine revelation because we know ourselves, love ourselves, is dreamlike. But the remnants of pandering—to whiteness and white gender formations—keeps honest Black theology within the Black church as but a dream.

I remember my mother, whose body was the roadmap for my own gender that defies white and colonial anticipations. She herself is a "marked woman,"[90] as Spillers writes, who will always understand me as, as Peterson lists, "the Belle, the Peach, the 'yes, ma'am' [I] need to be."[91] I am still working on not drowning under the weight of her language, and our A.M.E. church's lace head coverings. Eddie Ruth Bradford and Byron Cage sing two of my mother's favorite gospel hymns, the ones that she listens to as she

---

89. Cone, *Black Theology of Liberation*, 130.
90. Spillers, "Mama's Baby, Papa's Maybe," 65.
91. Peterson, "'My Pronouns Are Black,'" 1:49–1:52.

careens down the wooded highways of North Florida. Cage and his choir sing a triumphant hymn that compels every able foot to stand, women in white to stroll down the aisles, grand(mother) to drive a speed far past what is indicated on the limit sign a while back.

When the bread is broken in my palms every First Sunday, and I drink from the wine gauntlet, should it taste acridly to my tongue? Should the white lace that covers my feminized scalp feel funny? For whom is this pardon? If this pardon is preordained through the routine that has been etched into this flesh that is as Black as it is trans as it is queer, do I, too, get my blessings right now? Can I?

REFERENCES

Alexander, M. Jacqui. *Pedagogies of Crossing: Meditations on Feminism, Sexual Politics, Memory, and the Sacred*. Edited by Lisa Lowe and Jack Halberstam. Durham, NC: Duke University Press, 2006.

Bailey, Moya. "They Aren't Talking about Me. . ." *Crunk Feminist Collective*, March 05, 2011. http://www.crunkfeministcollective.com/2010/03/14/they-arent-talking-about-me/.

Bey, Marquis. "The Trans*-Ness of Blackness, the Blackness of Trans*-Ness." *Transgender Studies Quarterly* 4.2 (2017) 277. doi:10.1215/23289252-3815069.

Bradford, Eddie Ruth. "Because He Lives." *Too Close to the Mirror*. Juana Records. 2003.

Cage, Byron. "The Presence of the Lord." *Live at New Birth Cathedral*. Prod. Kurt Carr. GospoCentric Records. February 18, 2003.

Carter, David. "'What's Past Is Prologue'": Julie Dash, *Daughters of the Dust*, and Building a Solid Foundation for the Future." *Indiana University Cinema*, December 08, 2016. https://blogs.iu.edu/aplaceforfilm/2016/12/08/whats-past-is-prologue-julie-dash-daughters-of-the-dust-and-building-a-solid-foundation-for-the-future/.

Cone, James. *A Black Theology of Liberation*. Maryknoll, NY: Orbis, 1970.

Copeland, M. Shawn. "December 2000 Editorial." *Theological Studies*, December 1, 2000. http://theologicalstudies.net/2000/12/01/december-2000-editorial/

———. *Enfleshing Freedom*. Minneapolis: Augsburg Fortress, 2009.

Crenshaw, Kimberlé. "Mapping the Margins: Intersectionality, Identity Politics, and Violence against Women of Color." *Stanford Law Review* 43.6 (July 1991) 1241–99.

Enos, Tony. "8 Things You Should Know about Two Spirit People." *IndianCountryToday.com*, March 28, 2017. https://newsmaven.io/

indiancountrytoday/archive/8-things-you-should-know-about-two-spirit-people-294cNoIj-EGwJFOWEnbbZw/.

Fanon, Frantz. *Black Skins, White Masks*. 1986. Reprint, London: Pluto, 1998.

Human Rights Campaign. "Violence against the Transgender Community in 2017." https://www.hrc.org/resources/violence-against-the-transgender-community-in-2017

Human Rights Campaign and Trans People of Color Coalition. *A Time to Act: Fatal Violence Against Transgender People in America 2017*. http://assets2.hrc.org/files/assets/resources/A_Time_To_Act_2017_REV3.pdf.

Jordan, June. "Poem about My Rights." In *Collected Poems of June Jordan*, 309–11. Port Townsend, WA: Copper Canyon, 2005.

Lorde, Audre. *Sister Outsider*. Berkeley, CA: Crossing, 1984.

Malcolm X. *By Any Means Necessary: Speeches, Interviews, and a Letter by Malcolm X*. New York: Pathfinder, 1970.

Mbembé, J.-A. and Libby Meintjes. "Necropolitics." *Public Culture* 15.1 (2003) 11–40.

McBride, Sarah. "Alarming Report on Rising Violence against the Trans Community." *Human Rights Campaign*, November 17, 2017. https://www.hrc.org/blog/hrc-trans-people-of-color-coalition-release-report-on-violence-against-the.

McKittrick, Katherine, and Clyde Woods. "No One Knows the Mysteries at the Bottom of the Ocean." In *Black Geographies and the Politics of Place*, edited by Katherine McKittrick and Clyde Woods, 1–11. Toronto: Between the Lines, 2007.

Morrison, Toni. "James Baldwin: His Voice Remembered; Life in His Language." *The New York Times*. December 20, 1987. http://movies2.nytimes.com/books/98/03/29/specials/baldwin-morrison.html.

Perry, Imani. *Looking for Lorraine: The Radiant and Radical Life of Lorraine Hansberry*. Boston: Beacon, 2018.

Peterson, Zenaida. "'My Pronouns Are Black.'" www.youtube.com/watch?v=coMv8CYvQAA.

Philip, Marlene Nourbese. *Blank: Essays & Interviews*. Toronto: BookThug, 2017.

Powell, Michael. "A Fiery Theology Under Fire." *The New York Times*. May 4, 2008. https://www.nytimes.com/2008/05/04/weekinreview/04powell.html?ref=weekinreview& pagewanted.

Raushenbush, Paul Brandeis. "Dr. James Cone, Professor and Prophet of Black Liberation Theology, Rest In Power." *Auburn Voices*. June 9, 2018. https://auburnseminary.org/voices/dr-james-cone-professor-and-prophet-of-Black-liberation-theology-rest-in-power/.

Roberts, Monica. "2017 US Trans Murders List." *TransGriot*, November 1, 2017. http://transgriot.blogspot.com/2017/11/2017-us-trans-murders-list.html.

Snorton, C. Riley. *Black on Both Sides: A Racial History of Trans Identity*. Minneapolis: University of Minnesota Press, 2017.

Spillers, Hortense. "Mama's Baby, Papa's Maybe: An American Grammar Book." *Diacritics* 2 (Summer 1987) 64–81.

Sun, Lena H., and Juliet Eilperin. "CDC Gets List of Forbidden Words: Fetus, Transgender, Diversity." *The Washington Post*, December 15, 2017. https://www.washingtonpost.com/national/health-science/cdc-gets-list-of-forbidden-words-fetus-transgender-diversity/2017/12/15/f503837a-e1cf-11e7-89e8-edec16379010_story.html.

Weheliye, Alexander G. *Habeas Viscus: Racializing Assemblages, Biopolitics, and Black Feminist Theories of the Human*. Durham, NC: Duke University Press, 2014.

Ziyad, Hari. "My Gender Is Black." *AFROPUNK*, July 14, 2017. https://afropunk.com/2017/07/my-gender-is-black/.

Rachel Murdock

Afrofuturist Women
An Examination of Afrofuturist Philosophy of Religion in Music

WHEN THINKING ABOUT AFROFUTURISM, I wanted to do more research into the role of women in the movement as gender has so much of an impact on the experience of being Black. In looking for a way to delve more deeply into that intersection, I tried to determine what was at the forefront of the Afrofuturism movement, which was music. Musicians create aesthetics, and their music presents some of the most common ideas of the movement to the public. For this reason, I will be examining the music of Erykah Badu, Janelle Monáe, and Solange through the lens of Afrofuturist philosophy, with the intent to understand how these philosophical ideas of religion work in the context of Black womanhood. I picked these artists because they exemplify so many of the key components of Afrofuturist thought, especially Badu, a pioneer of Afrofuturism, and Monáe, whose work is fairly typical of the concepts and aesthetics associated with Afrofuturism.

I will start with the framework for what an Afrodiasporic/Afrofuturist philosophy of religion should exemplify. By the name itself, anything Afrodiasporic should be rooted in the culture and the experiences of African people and people of the the African diaspora. An Afrofuturist philosophy of religion should also take into account the principles of Afrofuturism, namely, that it is, "a way to encourage experimentation, reimagine identities, and activate liberation."[1] In addition to these things that are essentially the basis of Afrodiasporic and Afrofuturist thought, an Afrofuturist philosophy must grapple with established philosophical concepts, such as the problem of evil, the concepts of deity, liberation, pluralism, etc. In the case of this essay, these ideas will all be looked at through the lens of women musicians, as they are some of the most mainstream examples of people grappling with these ideas, and they explore them in a variety of ways.

The first philosophical concept I will address is the idea of liberation. Liberation is a key ideal of Afrofuturism as a crucial part of the ideology is that things like science fiction are used to illustrate a world in which Black people have transcended the oppression that has plagued them. This liberation can be seen in Erykah Badu's "Certainly" in which she sings about a "suitor" who is attempting to control her through questionable means. I have seen many interpretations of this song, but it functions as an apt analogy for the African slave trade in that Black people were taken, rearranged you could say. But once there is collective action and people "wake up," Black people will be able to have agency in the world they inhabit.

This idea of self determination and racial liberation is echoed in Janelle Monáe's *The Archandroid*. In this concept album, Monáe's alter ego, Cindi Mayweather the android, finds out she is the Archandroid and is tasked with leading her fellow androids out of bondage, making some very obvious Christian and slavery parallels. In an interview about the album, Monáe says in reference to Cindi, "... she can be the one... to change her community."[2] Again, I think this idea of self-determination and that people are not passively being liberated, but are active participants in their liberation, is integral to an Afrofuturist philosophy of religion. In this philosophy, people hold an extraordinary amount of agency in the happenings of their lives, and are implored to take action.

---

1. Womack, *Afrofuturism*, 9–10.
2. "Janelle Monáe on New Album," 0:30–0:36.

Racial liberation also has an element of personal healing that is covered in Solange's *A Seat at the Table*. In the interlude "Dad was Mad," her father speaks about his experiences of racism in his youth. While he expresses anger with the way he was treated, he also says he "was" angry, implying that he is no longer angry. This relinquishment of anger is a theme throughout *A Seat at the Table,* and I think it is crucial to an Afrofuturist religious ideal because one cannot transcend the bounds of their racial subjugation if they continue to maintain the mindset of anger and hurt that was characteristic of that experience. Not necessarily forgiveness, but the acceptance of the past, and the subsequent rejection of those circumstances as the status quo, is what is so necessary for personal progress.

This idea of liberation goes beyond racial bounds, and is particularly relevant when looking at the ways that Black women are seen and exist in the world. According to Womack, "This valuation of the divine feminine is one way that Afrofuturism and sci-fi are different."[3] Women in an Afrofuturist sense have elevated status, directly contrasting the more mainstream negative associations with Black womanhood. This idea is articulated well in an interview with Erykah Badu in which she says:

> "Maybe it's because as an African-American woman, when our image was looked upon as second class, I embraced it," she suggests. "It's a really big thing that's been instilled in the people in the bible belt in this country. We were taught to hate ourselves, and if you were a person who rebels against self-hatred, that's pretty political. I went against something that they had planned for us. If there is a 'they.' I'm not a big conspiracy theorist either, but maybe that's why."[4]

When looking at this statement, it is important to see its Afrodiasporic and Afrofuturist implications. First, she acknowledges that past and the ways that Black women have been treated. This knowledge of the past and the experience of the ancestors is crucial to any sort of Afrodiasporic thought. However, she also rejects that

---

3. Womack, *Afrofuturism*, 103–4.
4. Bakare, "'I'm Not Sorry I Said It,'" para. 25.

notion of Blackness being inferior, transcending that in many ways can be self inflicted if people buy into notions of their inferiority.

In regards to the idea of pluralism, I think an Afrofuturist philosophy of religion would embrace it. In reference to the ideas of womanism that are expected of Black women writing about religion, Monica Coleman says,

> . . .the trajectory of womanist religious scholarship has left me in a house without enough furniture. There are not enough chairs, couches, or beds for me or many of the black women I know and love. It isn't a place where we can be who we are in some of the most important ways we live—sexually, spiritually, or politically.[5]

The habit of religious scholars not acknowledging a variety of ways to exist, as Coleman points out, is not indicative of the way an Afrofuturist religion would function, mostly because a lot of the ideas around Afrofuturism involve transcending already-set-out boundaries. It would be antithetical to the already-stated purposes of the movement to set out more unnecessary boundaries for people's inclusion.

The inclusion of all people in Afrofuturist spaces is exemplified by Janelle Monáe's *Dirty Computer*, an album and emotion picture that traces the adventures of Jane 57821, the dirty computer, and coming to terms with difference as a point of strength. On a personal level, much of the album dealt with her journey of accepting her sexuality, and along that journey, creating a space for others to experience something similar. In an interview about the album, Monáe says:

> We come from dirt and when we transition out we go back to dirt. . . . We're CPUs, our brains are uploading, downloading, transmitting, passing back and forth information. And with all computers you got your bugs, you got your viruses. But are those negatives, positives, features? Or not? I think it's a conversation I want to have with us as a society, as human beings, about what it means to tell somebody that their existence, either

---

5. Coleman, "Roundtable Discussion," 86.

they're queer, minorities, women, poor, makes you have
bugs and viruses. . . . it's about embracing those things
even if it makes others uncomfortable.[6]

This sense of discomfort with difference is displayed throughout the beginning of the album, with Monáe asking for a higher power to take away the things about her that are different, but by the time she arrives at "Django Jane," she has undergone a sort of self-realization that she is sensational because of her differences, not in spite of them. Self-acceptance is at the forefront of any Afrofuturist philosophy of religion because such a large part of the oppression that people of the African diaspora face is a lack of personal love that came from centuries of degradation.

Coleman spoke a lot about the importance of not ignoring the presence and importance of queer people in the Black community when looking at theological study, but I think that the point of political difference is also a necessary thing to consider. Erykah Badu recently came under fire for her comments about "seeing something good in Hitler."[7] . Even though that statement was very controversial, the sentiment of love is important as it transcends social and political boundaries. In reference to whether or not she would retract her statements, Badu says, "But no. I would never take back a message of love. I'm sorry that it was misunderstood. But not sorry for saying it because it was from a place of love. And sometimes that happens."[8] While I may not agree with her, Badu's insistence on love for those that have different opinions no matter how wrong their point of view may be. This is not to say that people should embrace Nazis and Nazi ideology, but I think that in an Afrofuturist philosophy of religion, human life would be valued regardless of the possible evil they could possess.

The idea of people having the ability to be as evil as Hitler definitely was, per the previous reference to him, and this capacity for evil has troubled many because if there is a benevolent higher power, why would they let people do evil things? I will acknowledge

6. Jenene, "Janelle Monáe on Prince's Influence," para. 3.

7. Andrews, "Pop Star Erykah Badu Says," para. 18.

8. Bakare, "'I'm Not Sorry I Said It,'" para. 20.

this question by first interrogating the notion of an all-powerful deity and propose some possible alternatives that make more sense of this question. In Monáe's work, she acknowledges a host of different options as far as deities that could be at work. In the title track, she appeals to the monotheistic God that is most widely known throughout the world, expecting God to be benevolent and change the things about her that made her different. Later on in the album, Monáe describes god as a woman. This shift from a male savior to a woman that she is in search of illustrates the ways that people wrestle with their understanding of higher powers and the plurality that can exist even on an individual level.

In regards to the evil and how it plays into our understandings of a higher power, in "On and On," Badu seems to argue that people are part of the higher power. If, as this song alludes to, people are part of the higher power, that would explain why there is evil. People are imperfect and capable of terrible things. The aptitude that humans have for poor decisions was also part of the governing body of the universe. Evil things happening is much more logical, and feels less malevolent than a so-called benevolent god that stands by as bad things happen.

This idea of humans as part of larger deity is echoed by Monáe in "Django Jane." This idea of an everlasting spirit that we are all part of who is called upon as a source of support sounds a lot like conventional ideas of deities, but also puts community as the focus of its identity. These ideas of the deity simply being an elevation of the self fits into the Afrofuturist philosophy because, as I stated earlier, it puts an emphasis on empowering the individual and self-determination, things that are so fundamental to this philosophy.

In conclusion, these ideas are necessary contributions to the study of an Afrofuturist philosophy of religion because they combine the methodology of other philosophers while focusing on the experience of Black women, making a philosophy of religion that transcends both race and gender boundaries. In the words of Ytasha Womack, "While Afrofuturist women are obviously shaped by modern gender issues, their creations and theories themselves emerge from a space that renders such limitations moot. The main commonality is their individuality and a desire to encourage free thinking and end the –isms that have plagued the present and the recent past."[9] Even though I have used women to explore the ideas of an Afrofuturist philosophy of religion, the ability of Black women to transcend racial and gender boundaries allows for them to possibly come to its truest form.

WORKS CITED

Andrews, Travis M. "Pop Star Erykah Badu Says, 'I Saw Something Good in Hitler.'" *The Washington Post*, January 25, 2018. www.washingtonpost.com/news/morning-mix/wp/2018/01/25/pop-star-erykah-badu-says-i-saw-something-good-in-hitler/?utm_term=.3fdba8e1fb64.

Badu, Erykah. "Certainly." *Baduizm*. Sister Polygon Records, 1997.

———. "On and On." *Baduizm*. Sister Polygon Records, 1997.

Bakare, Lanre. "'I'm Not Sorry I Said It': Erykah Badu on Music, Motherhood and Wildly Unpopular Opinions." *The Guardian*, May 24, 2018. www.theguardian.com/music/2018/may/24/erykah-badu-interview.

Coleman, Monica A. "Roundtable Discussion: Must I Be Womanist?" *Journal of Feminist Studies in Religion* 22 (2006) 85–96.

"Janelle Monáe on New Album, The ArchAndroid." SoulCulture. www.youtube.com/watch?v=QjhRgMCyzOQ.

Jenene, Tatyana. "Janelle Monáe on Prince's Influence: 'There Will Never Be Another.'" *The Boombox*, April 26, 2018. theboombox.com/janelle-monae-prince-influence/.

Monáe, Janelle. "Crazy, Classic Life." *Dirty Computer*. Sister Polygon Records, 2018.

———. "Dirty Computer." *Dirty Computer*. Sister Polygon Records, 2018.

Solange. "Interlude: Dad was Mad." *A Seat at the Table*. Sister Polygon Records, 2016.

Womack, Ytasha. *Afrofuturism: The World of Black Sci-Fi Fantasy and Culture*. Chicago: Chicago Review, 2013.

9. Womack, *Afrofuturism*, 104.

Nathan Hahn

Iconography in Afrofuturist and Afrodiasporic Philosophies of Religion

THE STUDY OF AFROFUTURIST and Afrodiasporic philosophies of religion is crucial to the fields within religious studies as the African diaspora has made many religious and cultural contact points with cultures around the world and throughout time. While the field is, in many ways, in the very early stages of development as a study, there is a plethora of robust history and thought content to be explored. In order to work towards creating this field of Afrofuturist/ Afrodiasporic philosophies of religion, we must make a departure from the diametric model of Eastern and Western thought and create new models to understand the world. Within Afrofuturist/ Afrodiasporic philosophies of religion, it is essential that there be characteristics of reimagination of reality, destabilization of dominant tradition, and African religious reclamation. Within these categories, the issues of pluralism, theodicy, the suprarational, realism, and ethics must be explored to truly create a model with which to understand Afrofuturist/Afrodiasporic thought. Currently, I believe there is the possibility for significant development within the field of Afrofuturist/Afrodiasporic philosophies of religion in studying the iconography of figures within the bounds of Afrofuture and the African diaspora. Working to establish a beginning for the study of Afrofuturist/Afrodiasporic philosophies of religion, studying the work and influence of Black cultural icons will begin to provide a framework for how one might build a canon of the leaders within the Afrofuturist/Afrodiasporic movement and how the foundational ideals of the movement came to be.

In order to begin developing an Afrofuturist/Afrodiasporic philosophy of religion, there must first be a departure from the dichotomous framework of understanding global thought and philosophy as Eastern or Western. These classifications fail to include the possibilities within Afrofuturist/Afrodiasporic philosophies of religion and limit how the field interacts across time, location, and schools of thought. Afrofuturist/Afrodiasporic philosophies of religion require a new understanding of the world, and perhaps even time, as more fluid and dynamic. Also important to understand is that Afrofuturist and Afrodiasporic religious thought expands far beyond the bounds of the African continent. Contact around the world with different cultures, subcultures, and religions are crucial to the identity of Afrofuturist and Afrodiasporic philosophies of religion. In order to start constructing our framework for understanding Afrofuturist/Afrodiasporic philosophies of religion we must first depart from the limitations of past understandings that cast the world as bounded and rigid.

After we have removed ourselves from the rigid frameworks of the past, we can begin to create new models to understand Afrofuturist/Afrodiasporic philosophies of religion. To begin, we will explore how Afrofuturist and Afrodiasporic philosophies of religion reimagine reality to engage with the fundamental categories within the philosophy of religion. Reimagination of reality is crucial to understanding how Afrofuturist/Afrodiasporic philosophies of religion can engage pluralism, theodicy, the suprarational, and even ethics. First, to understand what it means to reimagine reality, we must look at the past, present, and future. As described by Ytasha Womack in *Afrofuturism: The World of Black Sci-Fi and*

Fantasy Culture,[1] "Black geeks" have been in the work of reconstructing reality for a long time through their engagement with subcultures in comics, games, science fiction, and other activities. Black geeks have engaged with the past heavily with the following of the steampunk genre. Mixing elements of a real past with that of the imagined, steampunk recreates historical narratives. These narratives counteract the oppressive force that history has had on Black bodies by recreating a new history. In this history, creators can cast off the chains of slavery and discrimination, they can create new cities, countries, and continents where race is nonexistent, they have the power to turn the past into whatever they please, and that intrinsically creates a new present and future. In the present, cosplayers are able to reimagine and reconstruct their identities into whatever caricatures they may desire. Perhaps it is a temporary transformation, but it empowers people to shed the limitations and stereotypes of their real selves and adopt the powers attached to the personas they cosplay. Finally, sci-fi narratives that imagine a future where Black bodies are empowered, or race as a construct is eliminated, are stories of hope that give a light to strive for. They inspire people to become artists, inventors, and scientists, to use creativity to reach the futures that are written about. Science fiction enables individuals to create pasts, presents, and futures that engage with the core of Afrofuturist/Afrodiasporic philosophies of religion.

Reimagining reality engages with pluralism, theodicy, the suprarational, and ethics in many complex ways. Engaging in pluralism comes through in many works of science fiction that begin to erase the boundaries of race and other divisive tags. In Afrofuture, works such as OutKast's music video, "Prototype,"[2] bring possibilities into the picture. Including not only beings from another planet but with appearances of diverse races and ages. Out of this music video one can see possibilities for the future that are not limited by race or appearance. In the same way, reimagination of the past contends with the problem of evil as it does not try to explain why evil occurs, but constructs a past and present where a real salvation

1. Womack, *Afrofuturism.*
2. OutKast, "Prototype."

has happened. This is the thought that informs works that reconstruct slavery and the Middle Passage as having underlying stories that are unknown to the broader world, but rather has an audience of those who have a way of seeing beyond. Imagination itself is the basis of the suprarational, granting people the ability to create pasts, futures, and even presents that defy common sense. For example, *Pumzi*,[3] a short film set in what may very possibly be an alternate present or nearby future, reimagines the world in the case of catastrophe. It creates a reality where, although universally suppressed, people are equal and, in the end, there is a Black hero who brings life back into the world. Finally, on engaging ethics, reimagining the reality in which we live is not forgetting or erasing the past, but recognizing the evils done and creating a possibility for a way out, or a world where such things are not done. Reimagination is crucial to ethics in Afrofuturist/Afrodiasporic philosophies of religion because while it is important to recognize what went wrong, there must also be a vision for what is right.

Also important to recognize is the action of destabilizing dominant traditions in order to make space to evolve and reconstruct them in ways that can address the African diaspora. Works of an Afrofuturist/Afrodiasporic nature cannot remain in the confines of hegemonic tradition. As they come out of historically oppressed narratives, they must break down the structures that are currently in place. For example, Jay-Z and Kanye West's "No Church in the Wild"[4] directly rebels against the normative structures of current tradition and destabilizes what is for the sake of what is to come. Granted, many might question what that may be, but embracing the uncertainty is necessary as we explore untouched regions and planes of thought. The act of destabilizing is one of the keys to being able to reimagine the world and so engages with the major concepts within Afrofuturist and Afrodiasporic philosophies of religion in similar ways. However, destabilizing dominant traditions is particularly important to the task of engaging theodicy and the suprarational. In order to overcome evil, specifically racial oppression, one must

---

3. Kahiu, *Pumzi*.
4. Jay-Z and West, "No Church in the Wild."

work to destabilize hegemonic traditions and structures first. Along the same lines, given the emphasis on rationality within modernist thought, destabilization of norms enables for postmodernist thought to emerge and rise above rational thought. West, in "No Church in the Wild," gets at both of these goals. In knocking down the hierarchy of gods and kings, West opens up a space for power to come from the space traditionally below. He is also openly revolting against the sociopolitical structures which have held down people throughout history. Afrofuturist/Afrodiasporic philosophies of religion must engage with realities of the African diaspora. In engaging realism, it is not to accept things as they are, necessarily, but to recognize the potential for change within reality. In order to make an Afrofuturist/Afrodiasporic philosophy of religion, there must be a destabilization and reconstruction of hegemonic traditions and structures.

The very character of Afrofuturist and Afrodiasporic philosophies of religion requires that they speak to the experiences of African diasporic people and the history of African religious tradition. Whatever experiences this may be in the present context, there are often streams that branch off into these diverse experiences. In trying to create Afrofuturist/Afrodiasporic philosophies of religion, one should attempt to locate those streams and draw from them. Studying phenomena such as the Garifuna, as Barbara Flores does in "The Garifuna Dugu Ritual in Belize: A Celebration of Relationships,"[5] one can see one of these old streams that has run through continents and time, shifting with the ground around it. Even the origins of the Garifuna are a product of mixing between African, Central American, and Caribbean peoples. As we look at groups like the Garifuna and others to inform how we create an Afrofuturist/Afrodiasporic philosophy of religion we are actively engaging in a pluralist activity of bringing traditions together across places and times. We also engage with the suprarational as we explore parts of African religious traditions that do not abide rational thought and act in the supernatural. In engaging with the suprarational, new ethical systems must be formed, as past attempts at rationality created the current bases for right and wrong. As Monica

5. Flores, "Garifuna Dugu Ritual in Belize," 144–70.

Coleman describes in her work constructing womanist theology, *Making a Way Out of No Way: A Womanist Theology,*[6] by bringing the past into the present and future, new ethics are formed. And in forming these new ethics, Coleman begins to create ways in which to address realism and propose methods for change. A way in which this theme has been brought into the mainstream is through artists like Kendrick Lamar and SZA, through their work "All the Stars."[7] Throughout the video and the lyrics, Kendrick Lamar and SZA refer back to Afrodiasporic and African culture through setting, attire, and lyrics, exploring and reclaiming African religious traditions in the modern-day religious and cultural environment.

Finally, now that we have established the ways in which Afrofuturist/Afrodiasporic philosophies of religion can engage in the discussion of philosophy of religion, we can begin to explore how Afrodiasporic cultural figures can form an iconographic canon from which to establish expressions of Afrofuturist/Afrodiasporic philosophies of religion. From works of various genres of media, the icons of Afrofuturism and the African diaspora have been able to create resistance to the largely white constructions of social norms. In order to begin an exploration of the canon of Black icons, I would like to take a look at the work of Janelle Monáe, specifically "Django Jane."[8]

Even at first sight, "Django Jane" is a work with strong womanist themes that shine through in the casting, attire, and lyrics. Using images of herself surrounded by Black women, and creating an atmosphere of power, Monáe immediately begins the project of deconstructing patriarchal structures and racial hegemony. However, what really brings Monáe into the discussion of being in the canon of Afrofuturist/Afrodiasporic iconography is her lyrics, as she speaks on her own experiences and the history of Afrodiasporic peoples, all while creating an Afrofuture. Monáe most directly takes on the project of destabilizing hegemonic traditions and building new power structures to make her platform. Criticizing patriarchal

---

6. Coleman, *Making a Way Out of No Way.*

7. Kendrick Lamar and SZA, "All the Stars."

8. Monáe, "Django Jane."

structures in the opening verse, she references the James Bond films and makes the statement that it is not only men who can be the hero or fill that role; women are fully capable of doing so. Finally, she suggests that women deserve to hold not only center stage, but the whole stage as men have pushed women aside for far too long.

The next most prominent feature in "Django Jane" is the way it reconstructs and reimagines reality. She talks about the criticism of media award shows being overly white, and highlights the snuffing of Black artists when she references her own work, calling for recognition of Black creativity. She also directly engages with reimagining both the present and future as female. Fem-ing the future refers to her own organization that provides opportunities to women in music and how women are already trying to take a step in improving the world. Her reference to Transformers is a shot at the sociopolitical climate in America and around the world which has placed people on diametrically opposed sides rather than unifying people. Finally, Monáe refers to African religious traditions primarily through her video portrayal of herself, and those around her, dressed in powerful attire that is reminiscent of Afrodiasporic dress. "Django Jane" is a significant work in the canon of Afrofuturist/Afrodiasporic philosophies of religion, and Monáe is an important figure to recognize as a champion of Afrofuturist/Afrodiasporic philosophies of religion.

As a start to creating an Afrofuturist/Afrodiasporic philosophy of religion, it is invaluable to recognize a canon of Black cultural figures who have started to create an Afrofuture through their influence in media. The many ways in which African diasporic figures push forward Afrofuturist/Afrodiasporic themes into the mainstream require that they are recognized for the work they do. It is also crucial to see the different ways in which artists and creators have contributed to the Afrofuturist movement. Even the artists mentioned in this paper approach Afrofuturism in distinct, unique ways. Although in this case all of the individuals mentioned were musical artists, there are icons in other genres as well, looking at how Afrofuturism and Afrodiasporic philosophies of religions are developing and how many cultural icons have taken up the ideas behind reconstructing the world with Afrofuturist/Afrodiasporic thought.

WORKS CITED

Coleman, Monica. *Making a Way Out of No Way: A Womanist Theology.* Minneapolis: Fortress, 2008.

Flores, Barbara. "The Garifuna Dugu Ritual in Belize: A Celebration of Relationships." In *Gender, Ethnicity, and Religion,* edited by Rosemary Radford Ruether, 144–70. Minneapolis: Fortress, 2002.

Jay-Z and Kanye West. "No Church in the Wild." https://www.youtube.com/watch?v=FJt7gNi3Nr4.

Kahiu, Wanuri, dir. *Pumzi.* Cape Town: Inspired Minority Pictures, 2009.

Lamar, Kendrick, and SZA. "All the Stars." https://www.youtube.com/watch?v=JQbjSo_ZfJo.

Monáe, Janelle. "Django Jane." https://www.youtube.com/watch?v=mTjQq5rMlEY.

OutKast. "Prototype." https://www.youtube.com/watch?v=uqhJfjbNuQg.

Womack, Ytasha L. *Afrofuturism: The World of Black Sci-Fi and Fantasy Culture.* Chicago: Chicago Review Press, 2013.

Justin Lennox

Afrofuturism
Young Thug vs. Travis Scott

FOR ME, ONE OF the most pivotal aspects of Afrofuturism is its ability to rewrite the African diasporic narrative by way of imparting to the diaspora a sense of agency. As I look to align this notion to beings relevant and dynamic to my understanding of the diaspora, I wish to examine this argument by exploring how Young Thug and Travis Scott rewrite their own narratives through their music and personas, which in turn reflect the narratives of Black bodies in general. This paper will investigate how the concept of Afrofuturism is embedded within the artistry of the two aforementioned hip-hop artists. More acutely, I aim to dissect the contrast between Young Thug and Travis Scott by examining the varying manners in which they reflect Afrofuturism through their work.

I find Alondra Nelson's description of Afrofuturism to resonate deeply with my argument. In a 2010 interview, Nelson defines Afrofuturism as a way of looking at the subject position of Black people which covers themes of alienation and aspirations for a utopic future. Often, Afrofuturist interpretations of stories mirror our own, while appearing dramatically different. The tradition of storytelling follows members of the Black diaspora, including the practice of griots. In a similar fashion to the griots, but with a more contemporary, technology-based spin, I contend that both Travis

Scott and Young Thug incorporate Afrofuturism in their verbal telling and recollection of their own individual stories. Through the comparison of sonic choices, motifs, and influences of the imagery of each artist, we as listeners can come to understand how Jacques Webster II, known as Travis Scott, and Jeffery Lamar Williams, known as Young Thug, utilize concepts of Afrofuturism in the creation of their respective projects to form a diasporic narrative.

To understand the Afrofuturist qualities of the artists, I will be focusing on Young Thug's album, *Beautiful Thugger Girls,* and Travis Scott's album, *Astroworld,* as case studies. Both artists' choices of production and practice in expressing their stories verbally in these works provide insights into how they aim to create a futuristic Black experience. We can begin to delve into their motifs, expressed in albums and mixtapes, from the perspective of those who reach toward more liberating futures due to their alienation.

In *Astroworld*, Travis Scott actively seeks to disassociate from reality and create a utopian world where Black individuals can experience the essence of childhood. He is able to do so through the theme of an amusement park he frequented as a child in Houston, after which his album is named. Much of the lyrical imagery and physical aesthetic of the *Astroworld* project stems from the realities of gentrification that took place in the closing of this mecca of fun for Black communities within Houston. Travis's project creates a world where representations of Black people's childhoods are idealized as a result of him experiencing the alienation of the Black body in society.

In another fashion, Young Thug brings Afrofuturism to hip-hop by creating a rap album entirely with country melodies, acoustic guitars, and a southern dialectic that mirrors the slang he grew up with. The very act of creating an album like *Beautiful Thugger Girls,* which was marketed as a country-rap album, further alienates Thug's identity by leaving his music in limbo. He exists neither entirely within the hip-hop universe, nor does he exist within the country universe. Yet, he has carved out an entirely new genre of music where he stands alone. As Thug bluntly exclaims in an interview he did with Clique TV in 2015, "Yeah, I'm not from here... I'm ready to go back [referring to an alternate earthlike planet]. This shit petty."[1] As Young Thug has expressed on various occasions, the artist believes he ultimately stands alone in this world, and all of his peculiarities in voice, and how he presents himself as an artist, make him alien and subsequently unique in this society. Unlike Travis, who wishes to create a space to combat the alienation felt by Black people, Thug uses *Beautiful Thugger Girls* to relay the futurist idea that Black people's alienation should be applauded.

A closer analysis of diction within the albums enlightens the nuances between each artist's incorporation of Afrofuturism. Travis Scott's outro to the *Astroworld* project, "Coffee Bean," shows him reflecting on his life as a Black male in a very white-dominated world as a result of his shift into stardom as well as his relationship with white supermodel and businesswoman, Kylie Jenner.

Scott manifests how he feels not only like a burden, but also like an alien within his own Black skin. He continues to reflect on this, talking about how a family of white, elite socialites saw him as just a dirty, ignorant Black man. Similar to Young Thug, Scott feels as if he stands alone in this world, but not necessarily in a positive light. Scott acknowledges the problems of being a Black male in this world, and actively seeks to disassociate through a futuristic recreation of Astroworld.

Like George Clinton and Parliament-Funkadelic, as well as other Afrofuturist acts of the time, Travis Scott is able to take Black people into the realm of space and different galaxies, which for a long time was exclusively reserved as an extension of colonial white imagery. Scott is able to project a more intricate, dynamic Black future. Through the *Astroworld* project, he thrusts the listener into a visualization of this extraterrestrial experience of disassociation.

Again, Scott stresses his need to disassociate from the realities around him and visualize something greater. His disassociation ultimately serves as a method of liberation for him, and in turn, a method of liberation for Black bodies in this extraterrestrial realm.

For Young Thug, the use of Afrofuturism is derived from his acceptance of being an alienated body. A lot of Young Thug's lyrics involve concepts around embracing being Black. For people in the

---

1. "Clique x Young Thug 'ATLIEN,'" 7:21–7:52.

diaspora, being Black can often be equated to being an alienated body. Thus, by embracing being Black, Thug is thereby coming to terms with the alienation he experiences as a Black body. In contrast to Scott's disassociation using Afrofuturism, Young Thug's Afrofuturist narrative embodies an aspiration for the Black body. In Young Thug's song "Me or Us," he, similar to Scott, reflects on his love life and sentiments regarding women. Thug actively represents his love and admiration of Black women.

Young Thug utilizes his own dialectic and makes listeners digest Black beauty in a different fashion. In his retelling of a Black love story during a time where Black love is viewed as an anomaly, Young Thug vividly portrays his appreciation for Black skin, and specifically Black women, through an analysis of motifs utilized in his music.

While the impetus for aspiring towards a utopic future may be different for Young Thug and Travis Scott, there is no doubt that they are able to express these Afrofuturist qualities within their projects. While Scott actively illustrates his feeling of alienation of the Black body in white-dominated spaces of society in an attempt to provide a different narrative, Young Thug creates Afrofuturistic content to embrace his feelings of alienation in white spaces and redefine Blackness in a positive light. Both artists stand alone, but create their music to different ends. Scott purposely disassociates from reality and creates a new universe for himself and others. In contrast, Young Thug creates a universe around himself within his own reality, working to redefine what it means to be Black. While both artists acknowledge the fact that they are alien beings, one chooses to redefine what it means to be alien, while the other escapes the feeling of being alien. A discussion of the effectiveness of each approach culminates in a common critique of Afrofuturism, which argues that many of the ideals in these futuristic spaces are contrived and like any amusement park that must be built up, it will always eventually come to an end. While Afrofuturism allows one to disassociate, it also realizes one must come back down to reality. Thus, I believe that while Scott's Afrofuturism is more palatable and welcoming at first, Young Thug's is likely to last longer and be more durable.

WORKS CITED

"Clique x Young Thug 'ATLIEN.'" *YouTube*, September 17, 2015. https://www.youtube.com/watch?v=wXAjHbs5cfY.

Webster, Jacques. "COFFEE BEAN." *Astroworld*. By Jacques Webster. Recorded 3 August, 2018. Produced by Ninteen85. Cactus Jack Records, 2018. MP3.

Williams, Jeffrey L. "Me or Us." *Beautiful Thugger Girls*. By Jeffrey Williams. Recorded 16 June, 2017. Producer Austin Post. 300 Entertainment, 2017. MP3.

Madison Barre-Hemmingway

Science Fiction Is Not the Only Source of Afrofuturism

LOOKING AT DIFFERENT SOURCES of religion from an Afrodiasporic and Afrofuturist prospective, I have learned a lot about the different ways that religion could be viewed. In a class dedicated to Afrofuturism and Afrodiasporic ideas of religion, we were only assigned one book to read about Afrofuturism. But why? After doing some further research, I learned the availability of books about Afrofuturism are extremely limited. The most common search result for books about Afrofuturism was one by Womack, the book that we read. Right away, her book started talking about the history of Afrofuturism in a scientific light and did not define what Afrofuturism actually is until around page 9. I was bored and lost within two pages. Of the few books that are about Afrofuturism, almost all of them are looking at it from a science-fictional view. Womack used this definition in her book:

> "I generally define Afrofuturism as a way of imaging possible futures through a black cultural lens," says Ingrid LaFleur, an art curator and Afrofuturist. . . . "I see

Afrofturuism as a way to encourage experimentation, reimagine identities, and activate liberation."[1]

This definition fits my definition of Afrofuturism, but fails to fit Womack's. I see a disconnect to where others view this definition as using a science-fictional lens, meaning imagining Afrofuturism based in an imagined, future, scientific, and "out of this world" context. LaFleur's definition connects to Afrofuturism as philosophy of religion, which is the idea of hope and faith. As discussed in class, because religion has so many definitions, we learned that religion could mean believing in a higher being or ideal or anything you want it to mean. But to most, religion is whatever you could put faith into, which also means that religion means having hope. Hope does not have to be in a specific thing or idea, but as long as the hope exists, that is religion. So, if religion is about hope, and religion is something you hope for, how could science fiction be religion? It cannot be made real . . . not in the next fifty years at least. I want to look at Afrofuturism from a realistic view.

In this essay, I will argue that Afrofuturist religion is a theoretical concept that almost none of the world has discovered yet. Afrofuturist religion is looking at all the hardships that Black people endured and endure today and using that to create a hope for the future. In doing this, I will engage multiple theses, such as the works of Cathy J. Cohen, Ingrid LaFleur, and Monica Coleman to support my claim. I will also focus on the experiences of Black queer people in society as well as Black identities. Instead of focusing so much on the science-fiction-futuristic perspective, I will stray away from Womack's definition of Afrofuturism.

Science fiction was initially necessary for Afrofuturism because, for a while, a future for Black people was not easily imagined; it was valuable but not practical. For example, in Christianity and the classic Bible story of Moses parting the Red Sea, it is challenging to visualize a man splitting the sea in half and creating a wall of water on both sides, freeing the Jews from slavery; at one point, a future was unimaginable for them. After the story has been told for generations, we still believe (have faith) in this story and hope

1. Womack, *Afrofuturism*, 9.

that it happened because the story represents the freedom of oppressed peoples. Just as the Jews had a challenging time during their slavery to visualize a better future, Black people also had an easier time visualizing a better future in an "out of this world" perspective. To put it in perspective, what's easier to imagine: Complete world peace without hatred, or life on Mars? For most, it would be Mars.

The inability to visualize a better future did not just happen out of nowhere; the oppressive history of Black people made it difficult to move forward. During slavery, Black bodies had to survive through abuse, rape, and inhumane conditions. The detriments it had on people are more than any book or source could ever explain. Coleman mentions that the past will insert itself in our lives whether we want it to or not.[2] No matter what anyone says, not remembering and acknowledging a past of pain and suffering is disadvantageous and impossible. You cannot forget your past or where you came from, no matter how hard you try. Your past is part of your identity. Where we, as Black people, are now in society is farther than some slaves could have dreamed. The Black community is building up slowly.

Recently, *Black Panther* was released and was a monumental movie for Black people everywhere. This movie is the first majority Black film, cast and crew, that has made the top-ten highest-grossing movie list. *Black Panther's* storyline is incredible and shows how Afrofuturism could be in present-day culture. However, there were some science fiction elements to the movie, like that Wakanda is completely powered by vibranium (a fictitious, naturally sourced element), this movie also showed what could happen in a strong, uncolonized, Black, self-sufficient society. This image was powerful. A community that shows each other love over violence, is not plagued by poverty, and is not constantly threated by colonization from Western society, is unheard of in our world around us. This movie shows an alternative reality for Black society.

Black Panther makes a strong contrast by showing the impoverished parts of Oakland, California, an area infamously known as the hood, by contrasting it with the wealthy and plentiful Wakanda.

2. Coleman, *Making a Way out of No Way*, 105.

When relating Afrofuturism and religion to the *Black Panther*, this connection strongly portrays that you must acknowledge your past and have hope for the future. Wakanda, as a country, is powerful because of the history of slavery and domination that plagued the history of Africa. Many parts of Africa are still considered "third world," meaning that it is underdeveloped and has widespread poverty. The idea of there being a strong economic and peaceful land in Africa is baffling for some. By comparing this efficient Black country to Oakland, it shows where Black people are and where they have ended up as a result of their oppression, but also where they could be or could have been.

With Afrofuturist religion and improvements being made in the lives of Black people in today's society, a realistic version of Wakanda can be visualized in our lives. Although it would not be nearly as wealthy, especially in the beginning, a new society could be theorized. Yes, our history does not start out as strong as Wakanda's did, but a goal could be to create a society similar to that of Wakanda. We cannot forget our past and compare ourselves to other self-sufficient, flourishing societies because they have not had nearly as many hardships as Black Americans have experienced. To create a strong community like Wakanda in real life, like Coleman said, acknowledging the problems of the past and problems of the present is extremely necessary.[3] Issues plaguing Black people in today's society, such as connotations with being Black and other problems, like the need for intersectionality, is so important in understanding where to go next to obtain a society like Wakanda.

Understanding Blackness in today's society has very similar connotations to what Blackness meant in the past. Black bodies are still overly sexualized. In the past, this view links back to slavery and forced sexualization of Black bodies. Pilgrim, a Professor of Sociology at Ferris State University, said:

> Slaves, of both sexes and all ages, often wore few clothes or clothes so ragged that their legs, thighs, and chests were exposed. Conversely, whites, especially women, wore clothing over most of their bodies. The contrast

3. Coleman, *Making a Way out of No Way*, 105.

between the clothing reinforced the beliefs that white women were civilized, modest, and sexually pure, whereas black women were uncivilized, immodest, and sexually aberrant.[4]

This quote is a strong comparison of the views of slaves and their owners. Slaves had no choice but to wear what they had, and for slaves, it was not a lot of clothing. Even if a lot of clothing was allowed, the harsh and long work days in the fields made it very challenging to wear much clothing. With this forced sexualization, slaves were also subjected to have sex with one another for their masters' enjoyment. This view still follows Black people into today's society. Because of the abuse of their bodies, they fit as "others." Black bodies are also unrepresented in the media. Viewed similarly and rooting from slavery, Black bodies have unchanged views from their white counterparts. Miller-Young, a Professor of Women's Studies, comments on this:

It speaks to the ways in which there's this simultaneous problem that was like a deep desire to have those bodies present and to consume those bodies as commodities, but a deep disgust for black people, our humanity and our bodies, at the same time that allows that devaluing to function.[5]

This quote connects to the need for the visualization of Black bodies for one's own enjoyment, but also to the deep-rooted hatred that leads to discrediting the need. This creates a scenario where Black people cannot do anything right; by existing, they are unimportant and seemingly unneeded, but by not existing they will be missed by their oppressors. It seems that Black bodies cannot be seen as more than sex objects.

When being sexualized, you are being dehumanized. If you are not human, you neither have rights nor a future. This constant dehumanization could be the reason that Womack chose to base her book as deeply in science fiction as she did. For a while, the

4. Pilgrim, "Jezebel Stereotype," para. 10.

5. Miller-Young, "Sex Stereotypes of African Americans Have Long History," para. 6.

world seemed like a place where Black people belonged because of the way that they were treated. Although not as blatant, Black people are still treated inhumanely and continue to have a strong need for Afrofuturist religion.

Black bodies in present times, especially in the media, are underrepresented and underpaid. Black women in film make half to three-quarters less than their white counterparts. If there is not representation in the media, the cycle of discomfort with Blackness continues. This issue rings true for Moore: "Race as well as gender expression made it difficult for her to see how her experience as a Black girl related to the image of Barbie as the ideal expression of female gender."[6] When I first read this quote, I hated that I related so much to this. I grew up in a white community and learned quickly that darker is considered ugly. I got to a point where when people would call me "she" or refer to me as female pronouns, I started to question whether I really was female and if I really was a person. My surroundings made me question not only my gender, but my worth. So, if I, as a straight, cisgender woman, questioned my identity and all that I know, how could Black, female-identifying queers come to terms with who they are?

Although it is not as grand as flying cars or anything that Womack imagined, Afrofuturism and religion, in this case, could be considered just hoping and wanting others to visualize Black bodies as people too. My experiences are not unique and there are many other perspectives with similar experiences of the dehumanization of Black bodies from other Black people everywhere. What many do not understand is that Black people have so far to go before we are considered equal to our white counterparts. Johnston says, "For me, it's part of my avowal that black people and Caribbean people are human, in the face of a world that continually tries to convince us that we're not."[7] Faith and hope should not be held in whether you are considered a human or not, but that is where we are. My Afrofuturist religious hope is that in the future, I and my children will be treated with respect and seen as humans.

6. Moore, *Invisible Families*, 34.
7. Johnston, "'Happy That It's Here,'" 208.

So, what about the experiences of those who are Black and queer, two areas of oppression that society struggles to accept? Black queerness is a societal taboo and is received badly by society. For many Black queers, the first thing that society sees in their identity is not their queerness, but the color of their skin. To state it bluntly, if one is prejudiced against someone's race, they are not going to learn or pay attention to anything beyond their race, including sexual preferences; it takes talking to the person to get that information. Cohen mentions this in moving towards inclusive queer politics: "Only through recognizing the many manifestations of power, across and within categories, can we truly begin to build a movement based on one's politics and not exclusively on one's identity."[8] In this quote, Cohen means that understanding for intersectionality is necessary for the queer movement to be successful. This idea is something that is not thought about or understood by white queers. Having more than one oppression adds a whole other layer to one's identity and how they view themselves. It forces intersectionality because intersectionality is not a choice; it is what society forces.

The intersectionality of Blackness and queerness is relatively new. There was no room for it in the past because of slavery. As stated earlier in this essay, slaves were treated like cattle: they worked and reproduced. Heterosexual sex is the only way to naturally make a child. Masters did not care about their slaves' sexual preferences. So perhaps, in this case, an Afrofuturist and hopeful view is for representation in the media and acceptance.

A hope for the future for Black people and Black queers is equality and representation in the media. It is so important for the next generations to have people to look up to. In past decades, I could name thousands of white people who were role models for other white people in my generation and the generations before me, but what about the positive Black role models? In the twenty-first century, society is consumed by media. Messages on the television screen are teaching our children how to think and act. If media is always hating on our Blackness, it is teaching our children to hate

8. Cohen, "Punks, Bulldaggers, and Welfare Queens," 458.

themselves. Gomez says, "A lot of young women, and women of color, didn't have the opportunity to read about heroic figures. They didn't have the opportunity to read about women of color who stood out as powerful and kind and yet were still growing up and finding their way."[9] Even in literature, the media of the past, young Black girls and women had no one to look up to. How do you grow up feeling empowered when you have no famous role models who have done amazing things? Afrofuturism is positive representation in the media. We cannot change ourselves to assimilate and forget ourselves.

Even if we did change ourselves for movement in the racial hierarchy of society, we cannot lose or forget our pasts, so why even try? An Afrofuturistic point of view is not needing to try to change ourselves, not needing to worry about going into a store and getting followed, and not worrying about our safety.

Afrofuturistic religion is so important for now and the future. We cannot forget our history, but we can use our history to imagine what our future can be like. We cannot compare ourselves to white culture or progression. They were not the slaves; they were the slave owners. They were given bank loans; we were not. They have had freedom for all of their existence; we have not. Dreaming of equality is an Afrofuturistic view, yes, but blaming ourselves for not being there yet is not our fault. As Gomez says,

> Young people commit themselves to capitalism, thinking that capitalism will save them, but capitalism is failing. The Black Power Movement was about changing that, until people realized, "I can be as bad as the white man can be." Afrofuturism is a response to that intensely negative sensibility. I see Afrofuturism as a sign of hope, as a sign of hope returning.[10]

Gomez is right: capitalism is failing us. Assimilating and trying to fit into white culture does not work. Capitalism was created to hurt us, not empower us. In changing and truly becoming our own people, we can have equality.

9. Gomez, "But Some of Us Are Brave Lesbians," 3.
10. Gomez, "But Some of Us Are Brave Lesbians," 5.

Science Fiction Is Not the Only Source of Afrofuturism

People in power, such as Barak Obama and Beyoncé, have had the ability to have their voices heard and progress the movement of Afrofuturism. With Barack Obama's inauguration as the first Black president in 2008, this created new hope in Black lives. He not only brought in representation and newfound respect for Black people, but also brought in a campaign for change. This allowed for Afrofuturism to reach a new peak; people were able to hope for a future that was realistic and not as grim as they have in the past. Musical movements, such as Beyonce's *Lemonade* album, also strengthen ability for Afrofuturist religion. She brought representation and beauty into the definition of Blackness. One of her most powerful scenes—depicted in multiple videos from this album—shows her and other Black women around her wearing beautiful white dresses at a plantation. This scene is powerful because it acknowledges the long history of slavery and has Black women in a position of power. This is a visual of Afrofuturism; a strong visualization of Black people.

The idea of Afrofuturism and the hope produced by religion are intertwined in the future of Black people. Instead of dreaming about what life could be like on Mars, now is the time to have a realistic future for us. It is time to reclaim what is ours and fight for what we believe in. Slowly but surely, that is what we are doing. We are rebuilding the empire that has been knocked down time and time again. Influential people in society, such as President Barack Obama and singer Beyoncé and her *Lemonade* album, have been positive role models for our youth. We are moving up. They are helping us keep faith and hope strong. Black people in power are trying to lift up those who have been dropped and forgotten by society. We, as one, will catch up. We are working to have representation in writing and in media. We are working to have more representation in high positions, such as in the worlds of CEOs and doctors. We are working to send our kids to higher institutions of learning. We are working towards equal education and opportunity. We are working. We are trying. We are building. Our future is just beginning and through hard work, hope, and faith, we will have equality.

WORKS CITED

Cohen, Cathy J. "Punks, Bulldaggers, and Welfare Queens." *Black Queer Studies* (2005) 21–51. doi:10.1215/9780822387220–003.

Coleman, Monica. *Making a Way out of No Way: A Womanist Theology.* Minneapolis: Fortress, 2008.

Faucheux, Amandine H. "Race and Sexuality in Nalo Hopkinson's Oeuvre; or, QueerAfrofuturism." *Science Fiction Studies* 44.3 (2017) 563–80.

Gomez, Jewelle. "But Some of Us Are Brave Lesbians." *Black Queer Studies* (2005) 289–97. doi:10.1215/9780822387220–019.

Johnston, Nancy. "'Happy That It's Here': An Interview with Nalo Hopkinson." In *Queer Universes: Sexualities in Science Fiction*, edited by Wendy Gay Pearson et al, 200–15. Liverpool, UK: Liverpool University Press, 2008.

Macklemore. "Same Love." *The Heist,* 2012. https://www.youtube.com/watch?v=0eLH0GOXlCM.

Miller-Young, Mireille, et al. "Sex Stereotypes of African Americans Have Long History." *NPR*, May 7, 2007. www.npr.org/templates/story/story.php?storyId=10057104.

Moore, Mignon. *Invisible Families: Gay Identities, Relationships, and Motherhood among Black Women.* Berkeley: University of California Press, 2011.

Pilgrim, David. "The Jezebel Stereotype." *Ferris State University: Jim Crow Museum of Racist Memorabilia*, 2002. www.ferris.edu/jimcrow/jezebel/.

Womack, Ytasha L. *Afrofuturism: The World of Black Sci-Fi and Fantasy Culture.* Chicago: Lawrence Hill, 2013.

Elijah Jabbar-Bey

Imagining and Actualizing Afrodiasporic/Afrofuturist Philosophies of Religion

Self-Definition and Plurality

IN THIS PAPER, I take an intersectional approach to exploring issues of identity, self-definition, and canonization that I find to be most pressing in the task of imagining and actualizing Afrodiasporic and Afrofuturist philosophies of religion. I stress philosophies because I believe that an emphasis on plurality and decentralization is fundamental for these disciplines—for their distinctiveness, longevity, and capacities to inspire radical free thought across the vastness of the diaspora. Scholars producing work in these disciplines must actively abandon the poisonous self/other dialectic for them to be successful in these tasks. By centering self-definition and plurality, Afrodiasporic/Afrofuturist philosophies of religion have the potential to develop themselves completely apart from the hierarchical binaries that constitute so many disciplines (canons of philosophy and others) and resulting counterdisciplines. From here, the power that these disciplines can channel for the diaspora is limitless.

The two academic works I will be highlighting to facilitate my illustration of these points are religious studies scholar and poet

Elonda Clay's "Two Turntables and a Microphone: Turntablism, Ritual and Implicit Religion" (2009) and Nigerian-born artist, curator, and art historian Olu Oguibe's "Editorial: In the 'Heart of Darkness'" (1993).

In her piece, Clay focuses on DJ-battling and turntabling as facets of hip-hop culture, which she ultimately argues are "implicitly religious" practices.[1] She invokes the theoretical frameworks of religious scholars and historians such as E. I. Bailey, Anthony Pinn, and Charles Long to define and contextualize her notion of implicit religion:

> At the heart of what religious scholar Bailey defines as implicit religion are commitment, integrating foci, and "intensive concerns with extensive effects." This definition emphasizes that the quest for meaning is not narrowly limited to that which is legitimated as officially religious; instead everyday life and subjectivity become vital to the expression of individual and collective contemporary religiosity. Historian of religion Charles Long in his discussion of religion as orientation, and religious scholar Anthony Pinn in his discussion of complex subjectivity, provide insights that are congruent with implicit religion as a quest for meaning through their affirmation of informal and formal religious forms embedded in cultural practices.[2]

It is evident here, and in the article in its entirety, that Clay's inclusion of DJ-battling and turntabling into the realm of religiosity is meant to illuminate the profundity of these practices and to generally uplift their status. I admire this quest and wholly agree with the sentiment that hip-hop, a gift from the diaspora, with its plethora of facets, global reach, and impact, is one of the most rich, cultural phenomena of human existence. It is precisely because of this that the language and framing of Clay's argument frustrates me so—serving as a counterexample to the type of knowledge production I envision in Afrodiasporic/Afrofuturist philosophies of religion.

1. Clay, "Two Turntables and a Microphone," 23–38.
2. Clay, "Two Turntables and a Microphone," 24.

First, I want to clarify my own basic understanding of the term "religion," which aligns with the work of Professor Jon Ivan Gill and his notion that, "Religion is a function of human life that grounds and propels us into the world based on that which is important to us—a means by which one constructs and ascribes meaning to the world."[3] Clay echoes this sentiment with her emphasis on religion's "quest for meaning" and how that includes aspects of "every day life and subjectivity," but her use of language of "implicit religion"/"explicit religion," "officially religious," and "informal"/"formal religious forms" reinforces ideological binaries that ultimately weaken her argument.

These terms such as "implicit religion" and "explicit religion," despite their intent, do not function as mere indicators of different types of religions of equal status, but rather this language serves to invoke connotations of value—"explicit" and "implicit" becoming interchangeable with real/unreal, pure/impure, and, ultimately, high/low. By continually falling back on these binaries and so persistently bisecting DJ-battling and turntabling (implicit religion) from the practice of Abrahamic religions (examples of explicit religion) for example, Clay ends up diluting her argument about the "religious dimensions of turntablism."[4]

I believe Clay's point would be so much stronger if she just introduced DJ-battling and turntabling as religious practices without invoking the binaries and speaking about them as counters or alternatives to explicitly religious practices.

As an Africana Studies scholar with a concentration in the visual arts, I consider including the voices and perspectives of artists of the diaspora to be crucial to Afrodiasporic/Afrofuturist philosophies of religion. This brings us to Olu Oguibe's editorial in *Third Text*. where he provides some powerful insight on the importance of plurality and decentering in academic work, pertaining specifically to the relationship between Africa (and the diaspora) and the West in this context. Oguibe expresses:

3. Gill, Jon Ivan. "The Category of Religion," 2018.
4. Clay, "Two Turntables and a Microphone," 23–38.

> Pre-modernism. Modernism. Post-modernism. For the West erase Pre-modernism. For the West, replace with Primitivism. It is tempting to dwell on the denial of modernity to Africa or cultures other than the West. The underlying necessity to consign the rest of humanity to antiquity and atrophy so as to cast the West in the light of progress and civilization has been sufficiently explored by scholars. . . . It is important to understand while counter-centrist discourse has a responsibility to explore and expose these structures, there is an element of concession-ism in tethering all discourse to the role and place of the outside. To counter perpetually a center is to recognize it. In other words, discourse—our discourse—should begin to move in the direction of dismissing, at least in discur-sive terms, the concept of a center, not by moving it as Ngugi (wa Thiong'o) has suggested, but in superseding it. It is in this context that any meaningful discussion of mo-dernity and "modernism" in Africa must be conducted, not in relation to the idea of an existing center of a "Mod-ernism" against which we must all read our bearings, but in recognition of the multiplicity and culture-specificity of modernisms and the plurality of centers.[5]

Oguibe's message speaks directly to what I find to be the faults of Clay's argument. By perpetually countering explicit religion with implicit religion, Clay is recognizing explicit religion as the center, the norm, and the standard against which everything else must be compared. This produces a dynamic that works to belittle anything that falls outside the boundaries of explicit religion.

Oguibe's message is also very pertinent to Clay's piece because in producing knowledge about hip-hop culture, Clay is inher-ently producing knowledge about the diaspora. The fact that Clay is analyzing cultural aspects of the diaspora through a fairly tra-ditional religious studies lens brings forth the tension between a predominantly White, Eurocentric academic field and subjects of the diaspora—very similar to the West/Africa tension that Oguibe describes. In this way, for Clay, explicit religion becomes the West—the reigning, hegemonic narrative—and implicit religion becomes

5. Oguibe, "Editorial," 4.

Africa—the vastly diverse body of ideologies and practices that must be discussed in its relation to the West. This is dangerous, especially for a conversation about hip-hop, which as an Afrodiasporic art form still falls quite low on the hegemonic cultural hierarchy scale. To talk about hip-hop and to constitute its value in relation to an external center (explicit religion—Abrahamic religions, Hinduism, Buddhism, etc.) is to ultimately belittle its significance as religious. The value of hip-hop comes from itself.

I want to take this moment to clarify that I by no means want to put down Elonda Clay, or her work in general. I value her work as an Afrodiasporic religious studies scholar. I just found her "Two Turntables and a Microphone" piece to be an effective vehicle for identifying some questions that I think are particularly important for Afrodiasporic/Afrofuturist philosophers of religion to consider in their knowledge production.

To conclude, it is important for scholars, people working in the field of Afrodiasporic/Afrofuturist philosophies of religion, to abandon this centering approach and the tendency to assume the role of "other." I want Afrodiasporic/Afrofuturist philosophers of religion to feel empowered to truly talk about what they want to talk about and on their own terms. We need not turn to the status quo, to widespread and often damaging narratives, to derive value or seek affirmation for the work that we produce. We must unchain ourselves from this double consciousness to unlock our potential. We are the future.

BIBLIOGRAPHY

Clay, Elonda. "Two Turntables and a Microphone: Turntablism, Ritual and Implicit Religion." *Culture and Religion* 10.1 (March 2009) 23–38. doi:10.1080/14755610902786296.

Gill, Jon Ivan. "The Category of Religion." PowerPoint presentation used in a class in 2018.

Oguibe, Olu. "Editorial: In the 'Heart of Darkness.'" *Third Text* 7.23 (1993) 3–8. doi:10.1080/09528829308576410.

Kalanzi Kajubi

Fela, Afrobeat, & the Contemporary Afrikan Gospel

WE HAVE COME TO understand the Afrikan continent and its history as it relates to the colonial structures that once bound it. As such, Afrikan history has been divided into three ages. The first was the pre-colonial. This was the age of Afrikan personhood, before the chains of colonialism ever took their mangling toll on Afrikan people and their culture, spirituality, society, values, and psyche; when Afrikan men and women could act and think based solely on their own volitions. This is not to say that all Afrikans in this time were free or even content; however, they *were* free to engage with one another, independent of foreign interests: particularly in the absence of racialized power relations. The second period was the colonial. This was the age of Afrikan subjugation and exploitation. Short as it was, this eon saw great change occur in Afrika physically, politically, socially, and spiritually. Starting in the late nineteenth century, European powers like Britain, Germany, and France illegally annexed nearly all of Africa into respective territories that were subsequently occupied and plundered for resources such as gold, diamonds, and rubber, among others. To facilitate their occupation, European powers fostered a culture of complacency among their Afrikan subjects by way of religious pacification and ethnic restructuring. Above all, they stifled the initiative of Afrikan peoples across all arenas of life, such that indigenous approaches to architecture, cuisine, clothing, political order, spirituality, economics, and a whole slew of other societal facets were mangled in favor of European approaches. Afrikans were forced to assimilate to the customs of a foreign world in which they had little to no agency to dictate cultural practice in their own lands. Notions of small-scale, consensus-based democracy, for example, were replaced in most places with large-scale, majority-rules philosophies of the nation-state, the grand multiplicity of spiritual practices were replaced with the institutional behemoths of Christianity and Islam, and so forth. In the wake of the Second World War, independence movements took wind on the continent and successfully ushered in Afrika's third era, the postcolonial, whose miasma we now find ourselves mired in. Though the political apparatus of colonialism has been dismantled, even today, six decades since their supposed independence, Afrikans on the continent and abroad continue to work to decolonize the myriad arenas of their humanity still steeped in colonial protocols, to retrieve those parts of themselves that were lost over fifty years of systemized dormancy of indigenous culture and spirit and imposition of foreign counterparts. It is this quest to recapture the Afrikan spirit, unbesieged by the baggage of Euro-America, that revolutionary Nigerian multiinstrumentalist, activist, and pioneer of Afrobeat, Fela Kuti, dedicated his life and music to.

From the independence era of the mid-1960s up until his death in 1997, Fela Anikulapo-Kuti wove the dreams and frustrations of postcolonial Nigeria (and Afrika) into enchantingly repetitive, melodic, sensual, and epically lengthy grooves that were never afraid to brush up against authoritarian regimes not internalized hegemon. Other than Nelson Mandela, he is perhaps the most recognizable Afrikan cultural export. Though him and his Afrobeat groove are most often recognized for their political commentary, much of the meat of Afrobeat is in its spiritual hinges, encouraging listeners to enter a conceptual space where feelings and emotions take precedence over words and ideas. In the wake of a spiritually mangling colonial era, in the midst of the domineering institutions of Christianity and Islam, Fela and his Afrobeat rhythm played a critical role in the revival, on a popular scale of indigenous Afrikan spiritualities:

> Music is a spiritual thing. You don't play with music. If
> you play with music you will die young. . . .When the
> higher forces give you the gift of musicianship, it must be
> well used for the good of humanity. If you use it for your
> own self . . . by deceiving people, you will die young.[1]

This music shit was not a game to Fela. He saw his role as a musician as being critical to the progression of this people and the functioning of their society, just as the teacher, doctor, architect, marketwoman, etc. In a social, political, spiritual, and artistic arena obsessed with emulating the West, Fela, instead, was bound, almost to a fault, to the quest for a psychological and spiritual return to Afrika. From 1970—the year of his self-described spiritual and political awakening—you would be hard-pressed to attend a Fela concert in which he did not dedicate a good chunk of the musical performance and obligatory monologue(s) to thanking, worshipping, and/or communicating with the ancestors and spirits that denote the Yoruba, Igbo, Hausa, and other indigenous spiritual traditions of the region. Virtually every night between 1970 and 1975 (save for the occasional off-days for rest, recording/rehearsing, and tour), him and Afrika 70, his thirty-plus-piece band of singers, dancers, and instrumentalists alike, would march through the streets of Lagos's mainland at the height of rush hour, touting and tooting their instruments in processions that mirrored indigenous Were and Ajisari musical calls to prayer, to Fela's legendary Afrika Shrine, an open-air concert venue in the then-slums of Ikeja. They would typically perform throughout the night, departing with the sun, giving a show that was equal parts concert, ritual meditation, ancestral libation and political rally, drawing on the symbolism of Afrodiasporic figures and philosophies from all corners of history. Just as the "the church is an ideological centre for the spreading of European and American cultural awareness,"[2] the Shrine was a space for Afrikans to explore, celebrate, and spread Afrikan philosophies of religion and politics.

Recognizing the systemized underprivileging of Afrikan spiritual ideas/practice, as well as the hypocrisies and agendas ingrained

---

1. Fela Kuit, in Flori Tchalgadjieff, *Music Is the Weapon*, 24:45–25:04.
2. Olaniyan, *Arrest the Music!*, 60.

in western religious institutions, Fela took it upon himself to remind his people of their spiritual heritage, to teach how to find beauty in themselves and that which spawns from them. In this way, he literally, revived (at least on a popular scale) the traditions of oral and musical traditions of history-telling and ancestral veneration that prevailed during the region's precolonial era. This in itself draws on the simple tenet of return, or *Sankofa*, which privileges ancestral knowledge and ritual as essential to informing ongoing presents and futures, values that persist (to an extent) in virtually all corners of the continent.

He writes a tune called "Suffering and Smiling" in which he unpacks and critiques the pacifying effect that Christianity and Islam have on Afrikans, to the point that they would endure immense hardships on a daily basis and generally smile through it all, usually in the faith of an afterlife of never-ending bounty. All the while, the spiritual leaders, prophets of foreign and inconsistently benevolent gods, live in prosperity off the profits of selling these dreams. He condemns his own people for smiling and projecting happiness even as they endure inhumane conditions. As he sees it, this is going into a state of self-induced slavery.

He addresses, here, the infamous problem of evil which has long troubled philosophers and practitioners of Afrikan and Afro-diasporic spiritualities. Simply put, "If God is so great and so powerful, then how is it that so much evil and suffering can persist in the world in such great quantities?" For Fela, the answer is simple: there are in fact many gods and many spirits, enough to go around! The issue is when people are forced, coerced, or even choose to worship the "wrong" gods, foreign gods. Keeping in mind the aforementioned centrality of ancestral knowledge, veneration, and geographical specificity of Bantu customs, Fela was trying to tell Afrikan people that it is their own fault that they suffer as they do, for abandoning the ancestral spirits from which they come, which provide them with lands of endless bounty, to praise white gods that have only ever brought them misery and toxic notions of 'propriety.' They were angering the gods, in a sense. If they would just return to an Afrikanism of spirituality, politics, and all other human relations, then their fortune would change. As he puts it, "Every race has a reason to be born. The white people have a reason to be born in Europe . . . they have their own god," and Afrikans had a reason to be born in Afrika "with our own gods and . . . mode of worship. But when the Afrikan doesn't want to understand or participate in the reason why he was born, then he becomes a failure."[3] Stringent as this ultimatum might be, in the context of newly independent, yet dissatisfied, Afrika, it was critical to revealing the selfish and unjust agendas that underlied this particular crop of Christianity; how it continued (and continues) to act as a pacifying agent in the face of neocolonial exploit; how it only seemed to deliver the type prosperity in Afrika as it does in Europe and America.

If I may add to the refrain, *Fela dey for Lagos, Fela dey for Afrika.* In an analysis that echoes Fanon, Fela concludes that the only way to actualize his own humanity as an African artist is by actively and constantly resisting whatever forces that systemically work to suppress his humanity on account of his Africanness. Leading a return to African traditional, musical, and spiritual practice was his way of doing this, even if he must reimagine them through new protocols. If we understand the precolonial era as the age of African sovereignty, then, theoretically, a truly successful decolonization would be a reversion to the precolonial, whereby African independence would manifest itself within the same complex and varied political and organizational frameworks that existed before European contact. Of course, due to the brutal extent of colonial contortion, this would be but an airy hope. Too much was changed in Africa during European occupation for such a dream to come to fruition. Languages had been forgotten, new ethnicities had been forged, much of African spirituality had been replaced with Christianity, and social organization and interactions had been altered with the advent of colonial settlers. As such, it'd be irresponsible to suggest (as Fela often did) that his movement was representative of a true recapitulation of African tradition as it existed prior to European rule. Rather, Fela becomes a prophet of a new kind of African spirituality, drawing from traditions of the past, but more encompassing in its reach. Every time he speaks of Nigeria he is also speaking of Afrika. Afrobeat in turn, becomes the

3. "Fela Kuti," 5:14–6:10.

gospel music of the postcolonial Afrikan metropolis, filtering the rhythms, chants, and melodies of indigenous Afrika through western instrumental arrangement, and furthermore through the urban dialect of pidgin English that imposes Afrikan grammar, syntax, tone, and idiom between English's soft and proper edges.

It's my observation that Afrikan and Afrodiasporic spiritual traditions and religious interpretations tend to be more tethered to material conditions, I reckon due to the great extents to which they have been subjected to vile conditions that spiritual/biblical notions of deliverance, exodus, good vs. evil, have far graver immediate precedent in their lives than people who are alien to such historically and systemically entrenched persecution. For example, the Nation of Islam, and James Cone's Black Liberation Theology in the US, interpret Islam and Christianity, respectively, with the very specific conditions of sociopolitical toil that Black Americans were facing during the mid-twentieth century. The plight of Black people can be related directly to themes/stories of deliverance and sacrifice that lay central to many of the world's major religions. We can see this embedded meaning in the slave spirituals of the South, and in the biblical interpretations of Rastafarianism and Afrika. The plight of Afrikan peoples is one of biblical proportions. We are still marching toward the promised land, we are still pleading with the Pharoah to let our people go, we are still waiting for God to trouble the waters. But until deliverance comes, Afrikans continue to hustle and squeeze out livelihoods out of systems that were designed with their exploit in mind. It's in reflection of this spirit that Afrobeat in the twenty-first century has embraced hustle as another tenet of its gospel, particularly as Nigerian and Afrikan culture is increasingly oriented towards urban centers like Lagos. It is difficult to describe in words the grand myriad of innovations of tech, industry, music, play, transport, etc., that happen in delicate yet chaotic balance in Afrikan metropolises like Lagos, Nairobi, and Kampala. From the little boys crafting toy cars out of discarded milk cartons, clothes hangers, and bottle caps, to a communications company like Mpesa innovating mobile banking in a society where the vast majority don't have bank accounts. This sense of hustle, urgency of life, is evident in the Afrobeat of today, with artists like Burna Boy, Wizkid, and

D-O. On his 2018 hit "Ye," fellow Nigerian Burna Boy interpolates a refrain from Fela's "Sorrow, Tears, and Blood," to articulate the miasma of postcolonial Nigeria.

In Fela's same dirty pidgin, Burna displays the ambiguous relationship that Nigerians have to ambition. In one sense, it is revolt, declaring that Nigerians and (Afrikans) no longer will stand subject to the incredible hardship that they endure daily. They will finesse their way to a satisfying life, someway somehow. In another sense, it is a conceit speaking to how, rather than standing up against the injustices they face on a daily basis, Nigerians would rather avoid confrontation so as to avoid any further harm. They cross their fingers and try to enjoy life to the best of their ability. Either way, it is an intimate meditation on the incompleteness, the hustle and hardship that denotes Nigerianness and Afrikanness in the twenty-first century. At the heart, both he and Fela are saying "We want to stop dying! We want to enjoy life like everyone else!"—simple declarations that, when sung and danced to together, result in somewhat of a spiritual catharsis. It places modern-day Afrika at the heart of the spiritual narrative. The gospel of Afrobeat does not confuse its listeners with metaphors of ore but rather places them in the middle of the drama. The book will never be closed. Practitioners and listeners alike will forever be involved in the process of sustaining and updating the African spirit. Somewhere in the madness of its broken English, endemic contradiction, ambiguity, driving bass, and enchanting polyrhythms is a complex and naked meditation of an ever-changing Afrikanity. We are still marching toward the promised land, we are still pleading with the Pharoah to let our people go, we are still waiting for God to trouble the waters. We no want die, we want chop life, wes till want turn up. One day, our time *go* (will) come to do all of the above.

WORKS CITED

Burna Boy. "Ye." *Outside*. Spacesghip Entertainment. 2018.

Clay, Elonda. "A Theology of Liberation or Liberation? A Postcolonial Response to Cone's Black Theology and Black Power at Forty." *Black Theology* 8.3 (2010) 307–26.

Fanon, Frantz. *The Wretched of the Earth*. New York: Grove, 1968.

Fela Anikulapo-Kuti and Africa 70. "Shuffering and Shmiling." *Shuffering and Shmiling*. Lagos State, Nigeria, Vinyl, 1977.

"Fela Kuti—Interview 1988 (Reelin' In The Years Archive)." YouTube, July 6, 2018. 19:17. https://www.youtube.com/watch?v=QtiAnjtYdwo.

Flori, Jean-Jacques, and Stephane Tchalgadjieff, dirs. *Music Is the Weapon*. Universal Import, 1982. DVD.

Ngugi, Mukoma. "'Arrest the Music! Fela and His Rebel Art and Politics' by Tejumola Olaniyan; Indiana University Press, 2004." *Pambazuka News*, April 20, 2006. https://www.pambazuka.org/arts/arrest-music-fela-and-his-rebel-art-and-politics-tejumola-olaniyan-indiana-university-press.

Olaniyan, Tejumola. *Arrest the Music!: Fela and His Rebel Art & Politics*. Ibadan, Nigeria: Bookcraft, 2009.

Ben Miller

Nietzsche's Conception of History and Scholarship in Conversation with Decolonization and Afrofuturism

THEY MAY STRIKE YOU as the most unlikely of pairings, considering the works of Friedrich Nietzsche were used as Nazi propaganda, however several of Nietzsche's ideas from *Unfashionable Observations*[1] glean new meaning when thrown in the mix with DE colonial and Afrofuturist thinkers. The purpose of this paper is not to bend Nietzsche's ideas in order to force some connection or corroboration, but to see if any insight can be gained by seeing how some of his critiques of Germany during the 1870s directly map onto Afrodiasporic thought from authors including Frantz Fanon, Ytasha Womack, and various African philosophers and historians. Nietzsche's favoring of destruction in what he calls critical history, his view of education as centered around liberation, his frustration with the regurgitative nature of scholarship, and his emphasis on the importance of creativity and imagination, actually support

1. Sometimes translated as "Untimely Meditations."

many of the arguments from Fanon, Womack, and thinkers presented by Hallen.

Nietzsche distinguishes three different manners of looking at the past. The first he calls monumental history, which describes viewing history as a teleological series of heroes and landmark events. Perhaps the (in)famous Georg Wilhelm Friedrich Hegel would fall under such a categorization, however Nietzsche does not much care for it.[2] He also takes issue with antiquarian history—an approach that aims to venerate the past, highlighting preservation of tradition as the way forward.[3] Finally, there is critical history, which not only seems to be the type that Nietzsche advocates for, but also the type most useful in the context of the project of decolonization.

He defines critical history as characterized by "bringing the past before a tribunal, painstakingly interrogating it, and finally condemning it."[4] Critical history approaches the past skeptically, attempting to identify the detrimental aspects in order to eventually have "the strength to shatter and dissolve" them, which he argues then makes room for new growth.[5] In other words, because Nietzsche was frustrated with the way German historians revered history and tradition without critically examining it, he promoted a way of looking at the past that had the intent of questioning why things were done the way they were, and whether these practices or ideologies are in fact beneficial. If they aren't, he wants to "shatter and dissolve" them in the name of societal progress.

The most obvious way this applies to decolonization, at least as envisioned by Fanon in *Wretched of the Earth*, is the necessity of destroying the colonizer in order to liberate the colonized. Just as Nietzsche's critical history necessitates destruction of certain traditions to move forward, Fanon conceptualizes decolonization as "reek[ing] of red-hot cannonballs and bloody knives."[6] He argues that the only way by which "the last" will "move up to the front,"

2. Nietzsche, *Unfashionable Observations*, 99.

3. Nietzsche, *Unfashionable Observations*, 106.

4. Nietzsche, *Unfashionable Observations*, 106.

5. Nietzsche, *Unfashionable Observations*, 106.

6. Fanon, *Wretched of the Earth*, 2.

one of his consistent metaphors for decolonization, is by "resorting to every means, including, of course, violence."[7] Fanon further reinforces his support of critical history when declaring, "you do not disorganize a society, however primitive it may be, with such an agenda if you are not determined from the very start to smash every obstacle encountered."[8] Again, here, we see Fanon advocate destruction as a necessary tool for decolonization, supporting Nietzsche's idea of how one should view history. It is also worth mentioning, for the sake of defending the purpose of this paper if nothing else, that Nietzsche was actually well aware of the utility of critical history for oppressed groups in society. He directly acknowledges this connection when explaining that critical history is the type that pertains to "one who suffers and is in need of liberation."[9]

On top of critical history's relation to the use of violence and destruction in decolonization however, it also relates to rewriting the dominant, Eurocentric narrative of history that excludes and demeans Afrodiasporic peoples. In Fanon's words, "the settler makes history and is conscious of making it," and that as a result, "the history he writes is not the history of the country which he plunders but the history of his own nation in regard to all that she skims off, all that she violates and starves."[10] Essentially, the history of Afrodiasporic peoples has been told by Christian, white, male scholars, and this has had a damaging effect on the ways in which Afrodiasporic people are perceived.

This idea of knowledge production, and who has the power to tell and proliferate their version of history, will be explored in further depth in the section on scholarship. However, it is worth noting several Afrodiasporic thinkers who echo this sentiment expressed by Fanon on page 26. One such example can be found in Professor V. Y. Mudimbe, who teaches at Duke and Stanford and is originally from the Democratic Republic of Congo. The thesis of his book, entitled *The Invention of Africa: Gnosis, Philosophy, and*

7. Fanon, *Wretched of the Earth*, 2.

8. Fanon, *Wretched of the Earth*, 3.

9. Nietzsche, *Unfashionable Observations*, 96.

10. Fanon, *Wretched of the Earth*, 26.

the Order of Knowledge, is "whatever field of (Western) scholarship one looks to—whether anthropology, history, literature or, in particular, philosophy—the portrait of Africa that emerges (no matter how supposedly 'scientific' the approach is) is as much a product of Western cultural priorities and prejudices as it is of anything African."[11] This speaks to why destruction of history, as Nietzsche put it, is necessary in the project of decolonization, as well as the tendency of scholarship to blindly reinforce traditional values, in this case the values of being, Euro-centrism, anti-Blackness, etc.

Although Womack will become more of a focus in the conversation surrounding creativity and imagination, she also speaks to how Afrodiasporic peoples have been left out of the story of history in her book *Afrofuturism: The World of Black Sci-Fi and Fantasy.* While thinkers such as Fanon and Mudimbe might fall more on the side of necessary destruction of Euro-centrism in scholarship, Womack might fall more in the camp of the new growth that is allowed to blossom once one understands that there is a need to change norms. She writes that her work helps to "unearth the missing history of people of African descent and their roles in science, technology, and science fiction."[12]

Nietzsche's chapter on educators reveals more connections to Fanon, Hallen, and decolonization. Nietzsche makes this connection obvious when stating, "your educators can be nothing other than your liberators."[13] Notice he does not write that your educators should also help you liberate, but that they can be "nothing other than your liberators," meaning he views the purpose of education to largely be liberation. So how is this liberation achieved, according to Nietzsche? He points to the "removal of all weeds, rubble, and vermin that seek to harm the plant's delicate shoots" as the answer.[14] Like his work on critical history, Nietzsche thusly understands a liberating education to come about through destruction of the toxic ideologies that a student harbors. In the context of this paper, the

---

11. Hallen, *Short History of African Philosophy*, 44–45.

12. Womack, *Afrofuturism*, 17.

13. Nietzsche, *Unfashionable Observations*, 174.

14. Nietzsche, *Unfashionable Observations*, 174–75.

"weeds, rubble, and vermin," can be understood as the normativity of Euro-centrism, anti-Blackness, and worship of capitalism in education systems, the plant as the student, and the delicate shoots as their green brain, susceptible to educational influence.

Nietzsche refers to his greatest teacher, Arthur Schopenhauer, as a model of what an educator should look like. The first thing one might notice is that Nietzsche stresses the necessity of a passionate instructor. He has no faith in an ambivalent or neutral teacher's ability to liberate, and thus to educate. He writes that Schopenhauer's student must be "in his pursuit of knowledge filled with a fierce, consuming fire and far removed from the cold and contemptible neutrality of the so-called scholarly human being."[15] This aligns with Fanon's vision of liberation inherently tied to "hot cannonballs" and such, in that both see a passion or "a fierce, consuming fire," removed from the neutrality of scholarship, as necessary for progress.

Nietzsche's frustration with the "cold and contemptible neutrality of the so-called scholarly human being" brings us to the connection between Nietzsche's views on scholarship, and Fanon and Hallen's views on scholarship's role in Afrodiasporic issues. As mentioned earlier, Nietzsche wanted a critical and active scholarship, but what he found in his times in Germany was a stagnant scholarship, wherein "many critiques are to be regarded as an effect, few critiques as a failure,"[16] with little to no regard for how the scholarship affects (or doesn't affect) real people and their struggles. Fanon recognized the immense influence of scholarship on society's values, writing, "the colonialist bourgeoisie, by way of its academics, had implanted in the minds of the colonized that the essential values—meaning Western values—remain eternal despite all errors attributable to man."[17] Here Fanon speaks to scholarship's role in replicating and proliferating colonial ideologies of whiteness and capitalism. Although Nietzsche did not directly implicate racism or capitalism in scholarship's wrongdoings, he came closer than most would expect.

Hallen describes many Afrodiasporic thinkers who focus on the way that Western scholarship reproduces knowledge systems

15. Nietzsche, *Unfashionable Observations,* 204.

16. Nietzsche, *Unfashionable Observations,* 121.

17. Fanon, *Wretched of the Earth,* 11.

and mischaracterizes Afrodiasporic peoples. For example, author Okot p'Bitek's book, *African Religions in Western Scholarship,* and Ngugi wa Thiong'o's *Decolonizing the Mind: The Politics of Language in African Literature,* both specifically speak to how scholars of the West reinforce dangerous ideologies and misrepresentations of Afrodiasporic folks.[18] Congolese philosopher and historian Ernest Wamba-dia-Wamba, former professor at University of Dar es Salaam in Tanzania, also addresses the negative effects of the production of knowledge largely being controlled by white scholars. He argues for the "deconstruction of the colonial legacy" by, at least in part, epistemological terms, promoting the "democratization of the 'knowledge process' so that what constitutes 'knowledge' is not defined by other cultures and so that the bulk of the population is involved in both its dissemination and creation."[19] Among other positive effects, Wamba-dia-Wamba posits this will lead to the "defreezing" of the peoples' "creativity," which in turn will allow "them to move themselves to the centre stage of history-making in our countries."[20] I will refrain from delving into this quote in full, but beyond Wamba-dia-Wamba's condemnation of Western scholarship supporting Nietzsche's notion of scholarship, the idea of creativity as key to revolution and societal change can be found here.

So why is it that Western scholarship basically ubiquitously mischaracterizes Afrodiasporic societies and histories? Ghanaian philosopher Kwasi Wiredu provides an answer. He points to Western scholars' frequent inability to fluently speak the African language of the people they are studying. The argument is as follows: because "a very limited number of Europeans became fluent in an African language . . . this ignorance had profound consequences (which also affected Western scholarship about Africa) for communications with and hence comprehension and appreciation of the African intellect."[21] In other words, Western scholars dumbed down

18. Hallen, *Short History of African Philosophy,* 92.

19. Wamba-dia-Wamba, as quoted in Hallen, *Short History of African Philosophy,* 88.

20. Wamba-dia-Wamba, as quoted in Hallen, *Short History of African Philosophy,* 88.

21. Hallen, *Short History of African Philosophy,* 22.

African philosophies and societies not only out of overt prejudice and underlying racism, but also as a result of not being able to fully understand them because their rudimentary language skills lacked the ability to express and understand nuances.

Upset by the antiquarian nature of scholars, Nietzsche felt that the unguided "occupation with scholarship," and "adhering to the principle of 'the more the better,' is certainly just as pernicious for the scholar as the economic doctrine of laissez-faire is for the morality of entire nations."[22] The subtext of this beautiful quote is twofold in supporting the purposes of this paper. First, it promotes the necessity of passion rather than objectivity in education, and refutes scholars' tendency to reproduce old-knowledge systems. While the bulk of my project here is comprised of taking abstract ideas from Nietzsche, or ideas derived from 1870s Germany, and applying them to Afrodiasporic ideologies, this constitutes one of the few times when Nietzsche actually specifically rejects the economic engine of neocolonialism: laissez-faire. Moreover, he denounces it on moral grounds, implying he was aware of at least some of the unjust aspects of colonialism and neocolonialism. Nietzsche's condemning of folks for worshipping history more than they do life should be understood through the lens of decolonization as condemning an admiration of free-market capitalism (honoring of history) overriding the way people value life, (not valuing life exemplified by not caring your clothes were made in a sweatshop with child labor, or not recycling for instance).

Now to return to destruction and creation. Nietzsche warns, "if things are not destroyed and swept away so that a future that is already alive in our hopes can erect its house on cleared ground ... then the creative instinct is enfeebled and discouraged."[23] This breaks much of what this paper is getting at into an easily understandable cause-and-effect relationship—the hegemony of neocolonialism and Euro-centrism must be destroyed in order to allow for the creativity that will lead to liberation.

There's no better author and influencer to refer to here than Ytasha Womack and her vision of Afrofuturism. Her book, *Afrofuturism:*

22. Nietzsche, *Unfashionable Observations,* 177.
23. Nietzsche, *Unfashionable Observations,* 131.

The World of Black Sci-Fi and Fantasy, could be (roughly) boiled down to underscoring "the power of creativity and imagination to reinvigorate culture and transcend social limitations."[24] For Womack, creativity is a useful tool in the revolution against a Euro-centric history and education because it allows Afrodiasporic folks, and really anyone, to place Black bodies in a world unfettered by the oppressive ideologies of whiteness, and in doing so, provides goals and alternatives to the current state of affairs. Nietzsche similarly highlights creativity and imagination as necessary for Germany to, in Womack's terms, "transcend social limitations" placed by an antiquarian scholarship. He writes that it is only in "the pious atmosphere of illusion" that "everything that wants to live is actually capable of life."[25] This directly backs up Womack's idea of creativity as a necessary tool of resistance.

Before concluding, it feels imperative to acknowledge the hypocrisy of writing a paper that denounces reverence of Western canonical works, especially those pertaining to the diaspora, as Euro-centric and overvalued, while simultaneously connecting DE colonial and Afrofuturist thinkers to Nietzsche. There is some validity to this critique, however I argue that my reinterpretation of Nietzsche's *Unfashionable Observations* as they relate to Fanon, Womack, and more, constitutes a form of destruction and creation—namely, destruction of the classic interpretation of this text and creation of a new meaning. Perhaps in the future Nietzsche can serve as an ideological tool for destruction, liberation, and creation.

WORKS CITED

Fanon, Frantz, et al. *The Wretched of the Earth.* New York: Grove, 1965.

Hallen, Barry. *A Short History of African Philosophy.* Bloomington: Indiana University Press, 2009.

Nietzsche, Friedrich, et al. *Unfashionable Observations.* Stanford, CA: Stanford University Press, 2003.

Womack, Ytasha. *Afrofuturism: the World of Black Sci-Fi and Fantasy Culture.* Chicago: Chicago Review Press, 2013.

24. Womack, *Afrofuturism,* 24.

25. Nietzsche, *Unfashionable Observations,* 131.

Desiree Leslie Rawls

Black Christology Is Afrofuturism

CONTEXT OF BLACK AMERICANS

AFRICANS WERE TAKEN FROM Africa and enslaved in the United States for hundreds of years. The power dynamic that was fostered between black and white people by white people persists today, and continues to inflict psychological damage on black people. Generational trauma is the process of passing the trauma or damage from a negative event to the subsequent generations. This phenomenon is present in black families with descendants of slavery, because even after slavery was abolished, those who were free still did not have access to the same resources as their white counterparts. This is important to take into consideration because slaves were subject to physical and psychological abuse, yet most conversations about slaves and what they endured are reduced to the physical abuse. Many slaves were beaten and forced to watch other slaves suffer as well, but none of them were allowed to express their sorrow or grief. Enslaved people had to repress their emotions, and then as free people they had no access to mental health resources. This led to what I believe can be called an emotional incompetence within black people, meaning increased difficulty with interpreting and expressing emotions. The emotional incompetence and generational trauma feed into and exacerbate one another, and it does not help that low-income communities, which happen to be populated by people of color, have poor access to health insurance and resources, mental health included. Despite not having widespread access to mental health resources, black people have been able to find refuge in religion and the ability to confide in one another. This paper serves to map out the purpose of religion and its meaning to black people, specifically black Americans. Afrofuturism is a philosophy that allows black people to reimagine the world without the constraints and confines of white expectations. The reimagination is essential because they, as a people, have historically been erased and written out of the narrative.

HEALING THROUGH PRAYER

American chattel slavery was a process that actively took the power of black families, generation after generation. Africans were torn from their land, families, and tradition to be trafficked by colonizers who viewed them as subhuman. Studies of African traditions and religions emphasize the importance of community, yet community for those who were enslaved was constantly ruined. Communities were torn apart when they were initially taken from their homeland, any communities that had formed during time on the ships were broken apart upon landing, and once again when they were auctioned and sold to white people, where they were then divided into house and field groups, and even now the black community is torn apart by colorism and the biased and unjust prison system.

Although there was, and still is, inconsistency in community for black people at the hands of the oppressor, there is consistency in prayer. Africans in America were able to combine African traditions with what they learned and interpreted from the Bible. Some Africans had concepts of holy books and/or literacy, while others did not, but there was still power in interpretation of biblical stories and Scriptures. For those who combined this Christianity with African traditions, like the importance of water, manifestations can still be seen in baptisms that occur in rivers. Slaveowners used the Bible to defend their power over, and ownership of, other human beings, whereas enslaved people used the Scriptures they heard and the songs they created for empowerment and hope.

While enslaved persons were not sure of if or when they would ever be free, some found solace in this religion that was modeled to them by those who were against them. They were able to rely on and find hope and consistency in religion. The belief that there was a transcendent power who was always present in their lives, listening to their prayers, and able to deliver was more than enough for some of the enslaved. Prayer allowed some to heal from their trauma and hardships because not only was the believer recognizing and confronting their problems, but speaking manifestations into existence to be handled by this transcendent figure known as God.

RELIGIOUS PROBLEM OF EVIL

The religious problem of evil begs the question of how God can allow evil if he is all-good and all-powerful. This stems from people putting all their hope and faith into this transcendent figure who is always around, ready, willing, and able to answer an individual's prayers. To understand the religious problem of evil, it is important to break down the three roles that many Christians expect God to fulfill. God is viewed as omniscient, omnipotent, and omnipresent, but these characteristics are what complicate the religious problem of evil.

Omniscience means God is all-knowing. While this seems harmless, it means God knows the past, present, and future, even the negative that will occur. This includes large events such as slavery, genocide, world hunger, and more individualized and personal events that are still impactful, such as the death of a loved one due to cancer. While a tragic event like this may take place in an individual's life, they may try to pray through it, but when their faith is tested ultimately, like the loved one's death, the question "Why?" arises. Why would God allow this? Why would God not stop this from occurring if he saw it occuring? Is God truly all-knowing?

In this sense, God is persuasive because he is aware of all events and circumstances, and because he is believed to have the power to answer and deliver in response to one's prayers. When the problem of evil arises with the context or belief of God as omniscient, people can feel as though they lack free will because their fate was already predetermined and known by God. While this may not have even been a thought before the tragic event, it arises as a realistic problem that can ultimately test one's faith.

To believe God is omnipotent is to believe God is all-powerful. This points to him having power over all people, animals, and events, including those that are evil. Evil can be split into moral evil and natural or physical evil. Moral evils such as genocide and slavery are inflicted by people on others, while natural events such as natural disasters and diseases occur naturally or even at God's will. When people suffer from tragic events or are living lives unequal to those who are more privileged, this can be moral or natural evil, both of which can be pinned on God. An individual enduring moral or natural evils may wonder why God is allowing these events to play out in their lives if he has the power to stop them from occurring. This may result in prayer for God to change the direction or path of life to bring in more positive and to limit or stop the evils altogether because he is supposed to be able to. This can cause an individual to question one's fate and control over one's destiny.

Evil exists in the world, yet many Christians believe God to be all-good and all-powerful. In the text *Introduction to Philosophy of Religion*, James Kellenberger introduces the five main religions of the world and further discusses religion and its intersection with the existence of God. Midway through the book, Kellenberger dives deeper into the religious problem of evil, using the context of God's goodness and power. Kellenberger identifies three propositions that work together to worsen the religious problem of evil, which are that God is good (Proposition 1), God is all-powerful (Proposition 2), and that evil does exist in the world (Proposition 3). Reasoning among the propositions, Kellenberger concludes that,

> If there is evil in the world, and God wishes to remove it but cannot remove it, then God is not all-powerful.

(Propositions 1 and 3 rule out Proposition 2.) If there is evil in the world and God can remove it but does not wish to remove it, then God is not all-good. (Propositions 2 and 3 rule out Proposition 1.) If God wishes to remove evil and can remove evil, then there should be no evil. (Propositions 1 and 2 rule out Proposition 3.) Since the existence of evil is hard to deny, the problem is one of reconciling God's being both all-good and all-powerful with the existence of evil.[1]

Being that evil exists in the world, there is no way for God to be both all-good and all-powerful. On the one hand, if God was all-good despite evil existing, then he just would not have the power to stop evil from occurring. On the other hand, if God was all-powerful and evil still existed, then he would not be all-good because he would be actively allowing people to suffer. Propositions 1 and 2 would only work if all evils, moral and natural, ceased to exist, but that will not happen in the near future, so a new philosophy of religion would need to compensate for that. Omnipresence means that God is everywhere, all at once, and therefore sees all.

Omnipresence, for many Christians, is a strong character trait for God because they can depend on God to take care of and handle their circumstances well since he should be aware of them. As a transcendent figure, God is believed to have qualities that humans do not possess, and one such trait is his unlimited presence. For followers of Christ, there can be comfort in knowing that they are never alone and are always heard and seen. This unlimited presence ignites hope in those who believe because they know that change will come if they continue to pray. With God as more omnipresent than omniscient or omnipotent, individuals can gain back control over their lives and continue to manifest rather than possibly being dependent on, or wary of, a transcendent figure during times of tragedy.

1. Kellenberger, *Introduction to Philosophy of Religion*, 119.

WHAT IS THE PURPOSE OF GOD?

Through examining the propositions that amplify the religious problem of evil, it is now clear that God's perceived roles and traits in his followers' lives can easily cause mistrust and wariness. Praying fosters a sense of hope for positivity and wellness to either continue or begin as a way to limit unbearable hardships. The trust in biblical Scriptures and stories is what allows people to trust and believe in God's abilities to deliver and answer to prayers. Since the Bible is what ignites the trust, there should be less attention and focus on the transcendent figure of God and more on the principles of Christianity.

With God as omnipresent, he is always around and aware, and black Christians can gain back the power and autonomy that they have historically been stripped of, therefore allowing them to at least partially heal themselves. They can read the Bible and interpret Scriptures to influence their behaviors and beliefs about their own experiences and abilities. Black Americans have limited opportunities in comparison to their white counterparts in this country, and limiting black representation works to benefit white people and strengthen the power and control they have. In reference to slavery once again, slaveowners openly used the Bible to defend slavery and their rights to black people. Despite this, slaves were able to take the same Scriptures, even if they could not read, and reinterpret them. This creativity and imagination allowed them to gain hope from their circumstances, but white people still tried to stifle them. As Ytasha L. Womack argues in her text *Afrofuturism: The World of Black Sci-Fi and Fantasy Culture*, the black imagination can be used as a form of resistance. Using the imagination to create art and make space for other black people to be represented and have opportunities and hope is a way of resisting against the white supremacist society that actively degrades and belittles black Americans. This translates to the Bible as well, because the slaveowners did not intend to have the slaves use the Bible in any way, and often punished slaves who were literate or tried to teach others. The resistance makes way for other black people, especially the youth, and can aid in healing and recognizing one's own autonomy. Taking back power and realizing that God is in oneself would be key to the new Afrofuturist philosophy of religion for black Americans, but even black Christology alone is Afrofuturist.

A NEW PHILOSOPHY OF RELIGION

Starting with reinterpreting Bible verses and singing Negro spirituals based off of biblical stories, black Americans have historically used their imagination and creativity to rise from their plight. In doing so, they have actively countered white expectations and broken from the confines of boxes that white America places them in. Simply engaging with the Bible that was initially used against black people to defend their condemnation is Afrofuturist. Afrofuturism reignites creativity, imagination, and hope in black people. In theory, an Afrodiasporic and Afrofuturist philosophy of religion allows black people across the diaspora to write themselves into a narrative that they were never intended to be a part of. In addition, this revised and adapted version allows black people to find God in themselves by recognizing the multiplicity of their identities.

BIBLIOGRAPHY

Kellenberger, James. *Introduction to Philosophy of Religion*. Upper Saddle River, NJ: Prentice Hall, 2007.

Daniel Savin

Хип-хоп [Hip-Hop]
Cultural Learnings of Russian Rap for Make Benefit Glorious Nation of America

THE 2010 SONG «Солнца не видно» ("Can't See the Sun"), by Russian rapper Basta, has—at the time of this writing (Fall 2018)—been listened to 651,000 times on Spotify. A meditation on the state of the nation, its lyrics parrot Russian government propaganda, denigrating anti-government protesters and criticizing those who emigrate from Russia. Throughout the song, Basta emphasizes values like patriotism, loyalty to the Russian homeland and Orthodox Christian faith, and implies that those in favor of the government embody those values while those opposed to it repudiate them.

Vasiliy Mikhaylovich Vakulenko was born in Rostov-on-Don on 20 April 1980, and has released five albums to date under the stage name Basta. The styles and content of many of his songs will be familiar to any follower of Western hip-hop: the gritty street tale («Урбан»); the obligatory ballad («Ты моя вселенная»); the aware-of-his-own-impending-mortality-and-coming-to-terms-with-it-by-being-grateful-for-having-had-the-gift-of-life-in-the-first-place jam («Сансара»). There are parallels to all these within the Western canon of rap songs: most of Pusha T's output, Slum Village's "Fall in Love," and UGK's "One Day" immediately come to mind in each respective category, but there are countless others. Few of his songs are as overtly political as «Солнца не видно». Nonetheless, the presence in his catalogue of a song (and this is not the only one) that supports an oppressive, censorious, anti-democratic Russian regime is problematic for the notion of hip-hop as a vehicle for resistance against precisely those tendencies.

Basta is white but, being a rapper, he undoubtedly operates within an Afrodiasporic cultural sphere. Hip-hop has, from its inception, characterized itself as the vital cultural arm of the Black liberation movement. ELUCID, on "pure scientific intelligence (quantum)," the fourth song on Milo's 2018 album *budding ornithologists are weary of tired analogies*, is an exceptional autobiographical example of hip-hop playing the role of liberation. He may be talking about himself, but his bars could equally describe hip-hop as a whole, which is Black liberation put into practice. For this reason, hip-hop has come to be associated with what might be termed progressive politics. This tendency is so pronounced through the history of hip-hop that there are far more examples than counterexamples: from cool classics like Grandmaster Flash and the Furious Five's *The Message* or most of Public Enemy's output, to corny contemporary stuff like J. Cole's album-length crusade against sin on *KOD* or Hopsin's entire catalogue. Each of these, in their own unique way, belong within a liberating, progressive political tradition. To find counterexamples within American hip-hop culture, one has to broaden the net to include slightly weird and unsatisfying cases such as Kanye West's brief, bizarre flirtation with Donald Trump. Even that, in West's own telling, was a strange and seemingly misguided attempt to advance the cause of Black liberation. So American hip-hop lacks clear instances of the artform supporting oppression. Luckily for this paper (though it is very much unlucky for the world at large), Russian hip-hop has plenty.

When Brand Nubian's Lord Jamar suggested in 2013 that white rappers were "guests" in hip-hop, his comments were met with some controversy, but his broader point—that hip-hop remains a primarily Black form of expression—rang true. The history of rap in Russia is, therefore, fascinating. Here, after all, is a country of some 145 million people, with an estimated Black population of roughly 40,000. Because of the unique circumstances of Black

Russians (most are the children of those who participated in a Soviet-era scheme to provide free university education to African students, who then returned to their home countries, leaving a generation of widely dispersed self-described Afro-Russians. Because of these unique circumstances, Black Russians have little in the way of a unifying grassroots culture. In any case, the Russian rap scene is overwhelmingly white. This is probably a reflection of the lack of racial diversity in the country as a whole, but it has resulted in a somewhat bizarre local rap scene. A cynic might argue that Russian rap is simply transplanted wholesale from its American predecessor, but shorn of the sociopolitical and racial contexts that gave American hip-hop its vitality. Such a view certainly explains some of the more peculiar aspects of the hip-hop scene in Russia today: for instance, the utterly baffling practice of including some English-language verses in Russian rap songs. The English language skills of these rappers are—almost without exception—atrocious, and the content of the verses, constrained by the limits of the rappers' knowledge of English, is often subtly hilarious in its slight misunderstandings of the nuances of the language. For a full-length example of this phenomenon, see the song "Russian Paradise," by AK-47 and Basta (under the name Noggano), which is rapped entirely in faintly hilarious English). FFM Freestyle's "Rocket" is a highly amusing example of an attempt at imitating US trap.

Nonetheless, such a view is overly simplistic: in fact, these American influences have mixed with some uniquely Russian ones to produce the current culture. The song "Russian Paradise," for instance, though its lyrics are in English, has an unmistakably Russian beat that is reminiscent of hit Soviet songs from the 1960s. The viral video "Ty kto takoy? Davay, do svidaniya!" shows a traditional meykhana performance at a wedding in Azerbaijan. This is a traditional folk activity that is very similar to rap battles, but which is much older; the two traditions appear to have developed independently of one another. The battle is in three different languages, but the Russian-language hook, which roughly translates to "Who are you? Come on, bye bye," was the part that went viral around the Russian-speaking world (the Youtube video has 20 million views) and inspired remixes, parodies, memes, and even political protest slogans. One of those remixes, by the rapper Timati, racked up 10 million views on YouTube. Timati has collaborated with Snoop Dogg, P. Diddy (as he was known at the time), Timbaland, and others. One of his first hit songs was called "V Klube" ("In Da Club") and is very similar in style and lyrical content to 50 Cent's earlier song of the same name. In other words, Timati is the perfect example of a Russian rapper who is influenced by the American origins of the culture, but even he found resonance in this traditional, authentically Russian style of rapping. This supports the idea that the history of Russian rap amounts to more than the wholesale copying of an originally African-American culture.

By his own admission, Timati grew up with extremely wealthy parents. Oxxxymiron, another popular Russian rapper, holds a degree in Middle English literature from the University of Oxford. Clearly, Russian rap does not accord with the self-image cultured by American hip-hop of a method for the poor, disadvantaged and underprivileged to break out of their circumstances and achieve success. On the contrary, Russian rap is yet another way of further calcifying the economic and other inequalities that are already depressingly prevalent in the country's society.

Timati has been pictured grinning with Putin. Basta has made songs in favor of his policies. In America, hip-hop has always been a means of resistance to the government and establishment: one need think only of the cover of Kendrick Lamar's "To Pimp A Butterfly," which represents a radical claim for attention and acceptance, rap culture and Black culture seizing historically closed spaces for itself. Kanye West's insistence that "George Bush doesn't care about black people"[1] was a genuinely powerful form of resistance, and of holding the government to account. In Russia, it is the exact opposite: hip-hop is the government's faithful lapdog. Following a series of cancellations of a controversial rapper's concerts, Vladimir Putin recently declared that the Kremlin should be leading the way in youth culture rather than seeking to control or ban it. This might seem akin to the corny failure of the "Just Say No" movement to get a foothold within American rap culture, but it seems like the

---

1. "Kanye West Once Said (Part 1)," 0:37–0:38.

Kremlin enjoys genuine and enthusiastic support amongst the youth in the Russian underground in a way that the White House never has in the American subculture, and hip-hop is one of the ways it uses this support to further its aims.

American responses to hip-hop culture have historically fallen into a binary that is depressingly free of nuance. On one side are the true believers who will defend anything and everything about hip-hop culture. On the other are those who are intractably opposed to hip-hop culture, their criticisms verging on dogwhistle racism. Russian rap provides a fresh perspective through which to look at American hip-hop culture, enabling a more nuanced debate that reflects the complexities of the subject matter. Specifically, it tells us that the aesthetic of hip-hop is not inherently liberating, given that it has been used in Russia to perpetuate oppressive narratives and support illiberal positions. There are some American parallels to some aspects of Russian rap that are discussed above. Drake's privileged upbringing, for instance, is well documented, as is the shameful history of misogyny and homophobia within hip-hop culture. Overt support for oppressive political regimes is, however, unique to Russian rap. The fact that the artform of hip-hop can be used to advance these messages proves that it is not inherently freeing. That is not to say, of course, that hip-hop cannot support progressive and liberating messages. It can. Noname, Princess Nokia, Kendrick Lamar, JPEGMAFIA and countless others offer a unique example of the power of hip-hop in that regard. What the experience of Russian rap does show, however, is that rap is not liberating by default; it allows us to preserve and celebrate the liberating power of the music of the artists listed above, while also providing scope to criticize those aspects of hip-hop which are complicit in oppression rather than embodying resistance.

BIBLIOGRAPHY

"Kanye West Once Said (Part 1)." *YouTube*, July 14, 2021. https://www.youtube.com/watch?v=p9RtcklL0as&list=RDUJUNTcOGeSw&start_radio=1.

Magali Ngouabou

The Rebellious Nature of Christian Rap and Hip Hop

Salvation Is for the Broken

MUCH OF THE AMERICAN diaspora has embraced the Christian religion. As much as 79 percent of Black Americans identify as Christian.[1] Considering the history of Christianity as it relates to all forms and shapes of color, it can be difficult, from an outside perspective, to see why these historically oppressed bodies have internalized a system of belief formerly used to subjugate them. Additionally, what can be said about the majority of African Americans who take this internalization a step further and believe that hip-hop culture has a negative influence on the diaspora? Hip-hop has been a medium for the diaspora to not only vent its frustrations with the systemic undermining of Black bodies, but to build an identity that is viewed as valid and worthy of respect. Defining that identity within an American context has manifested itself in many modes of, and personal tweaks to, hip-hop culture, the most interesting of which has been Christian rap and hip-hop.

In many ways Christian hip-hop is a form of rebellion to both facets of its title. This paper will examine the both the rebellious and conducive aspects of the quasipluralist practice of Christian rap

2. Masci et al., "Black Americans," para. 2.

and hip-hop, and examine how it redefines both of its titular facets. All this in the hopes of coming to a conclusion about the role of Christianity in the diaspora and the extent to which hip-hop is an essential element of futurism.

A close friend of mine has always told me there are three different ways to proselytize or fulfill the missional aspect of Christianity: 1) knocking on doors and telling people what they should believe, 2) publicly shaming nonbelievers, and (you may notice a difference with this one) 3) living your truth and hoping people will find inspiration in your lifestyle. There by no means is a scholarly basis for these categories, but in a colloquial, familiar sense, they hold true. At its core, Christianity is about the birth, existence, and sacrifice of Jesus Christ, and everything between. The intermediate facets emphasize living life in a way that honors this sacrifice and the figure who made it, by proselytizing about how and why he lived and died. This thus brings us to the ways in which Christians are tasked (or take it upon themselves, depending on how you view it) to spread the gospel. Some Americans have probably experienced category one before, the world's populations have been exposed to category two on some political level (whether conscious of it or not), and anyone with a close Christian friend, especially as a nonreligious person, can appraise the merits of category three. But these examples do not even begin to encapsulate the ways in which missional services are confronted, and, probably, neither do (though insightful) my friend's impromptu categories. Professing the Christian truth takes many shapes and volumes, to varying degrees of success, with the most interesting method of Christian proselytization coming in the form of art.

Christian rap itself is not a recent phenomenon, but the popularity of songs with a primarily Christian focus has only become a phenomenon in the past half decade. Two of the biggest categorically Christian rappers today, Lecrae and NF (though the former somewhat rejects the title—a concept we will later explore), have topped the *Billboard 200* several times, but only starting to do so in 2014.[2] Before that there were the lesser-known groups who would

2. Green, "Lecrae."

play for the kids at Bible school, going on about how Jesus is your best friend, or some gems (like T-Bone, bless his soul) rapping about how he has been fighting to defend God's honor. The early 2000s were rough for everyone.

Burgeoning without much schema for how to make genuinely accessible and approachable Christian rap, Lecrae and NF (Nathan Feuerstein) emerged on the side favoring more traditional rap elements than that which had been previously established specifically for Christian rap. Rap and hip-hop are difficult to describe, much less define. Nineties-era Bronx rapper KRS-ONE argues that rap is something one does and hip-hop is how one lives. This concept of hip-hop culture as a mode of living pushes at the seams of religion, and the insertion of Lecrae and NF into the system of poetry, struggle, and creativity demarcated by popular hip-hop culture presents a complex approach to human religious systems.

Religion has different implications depending on the theological purview of the appraiser; therefore, defining it outside of human biases has been met with several hurdles of its own. From a non-Judeo-Christian-centric point of view, religion can be summarized as, "a push, whether ill-defined or conscious, toward some sort of ultimacy and transcendence that will provide norms and power for the rest of life."[3] Hip-hop, in many ways, can arguably fulfill these criteria. Referring to many a hip-hop lyric and artist, "transcendence" in hip-hop is achieving greatness, or, as Eminem puts it, simply being the greatest. This ascendency within the hip-hop community can also be seen through the various forms of self-evangelization found in rap music. Kanye refers to himself as "yeezy," Drake refers to himself as "6 God," Travis Scott made an album built on the concept of a world by and of himself (*Astroworld*), Eminem has a song titled "Rap God," and those are just some of the most prominent examples. This ascendence to greatness can further be viewed in rappers' lyrics, their expensive garb meant to show attainment of greater economic standing, and, in most cases, how they speak in popular media (in both subject matter and in incorporating elements of AAVE—African American Vernacular English).

---

3. King, *Encyclopedia of Religion*, 7695.

These elements are also why rap has been viewed as "detrimental" or "damaging"[4] as it can manifest itself through objectification, as well as misogynistic and excessively materialistic ways. Interestingly, many rappers identify as Christian or (at least) believers in Christ, and this, too, seeps into their lyrics on occasion. This introduces the discourse of what makes a Christian rapper different from a rapper who is Christian (and does not necessarily center their art around Christianity), and the historical and cultural implications this distinction has.

Christianity has a long, dark history with Black bodies, so it is no wonder that it comes into conflict with something founded and predominantly perpetuated by these same bodies. Just to name some of the conflicts: Christianity has historically tried to subjugate Black bodies, rap historically endorses anti-Christian habits such as engaging in extramarital and premarital intercourse, and often there is a blatant lack of humility, another revered Christian tenet. And these are somewhat superficial issues (superficial in that they are tangible and can be pointed to in any given competent history book); this is not yet even addressing the issue of discourse on hip-hop going beyond culture and into the realm of religion.

The violence historically executed on Afrodiasporic bodies by Judeo-Christian bodies is overtly combatted in rap music. Black bodies expressing a transcendent level of self-love is inherently combatting the self-hatred cultivated by a history of being denied humanity and the rights demarcating that humanity. It is undeniable that it subjects other bodies in its ascendance, but denying the ascendance itself is being willfully ignorant.

What makes hip-hop more than culture, as it dares to dip its toe in the dimension of religion, is the dimensions it has crossed and continues to cross. Hip-hop has transcended race, nationality, and even existing religious systems themselves, and has created a universal community in a way only associated with deities. No other form of music has started in one western concept of race and spread its influence, without being heralded by a dominant sociopolitical group, to other facets of humanity as potently as hip-hop has.

---

4. Williams, "Redefining What It Means," 4, 5.

When faced with the historical and theological barriers between Christianity and hip-hop, it is a wonder that there are not just rappers who are Christian, but Christians who have centered the art of rap almost completely on their faith. With the former, the rappers who are Christian, their existence and success can be explained by examining how they navigate this pluralism as duality, keeping Christian values or refashioning them to incorporate who they are in their rap lyrics (say, recognizing themselves as sinners but maybe not repenting as strongly as they could). There are also Bailey's definition and Clay's elaboration of hip-hop as implicit religion whereby commitment, having foci, and working toward these in the hopes of excessive effects, are more central than defined practices: "This definition emphasises that the quest for meaning is not narrowly limited to that which is legitimated as officially religious; instead, everyday life and subjectivity become vital to the expression of individual and collective contemporary religiosity."[5] Though Christianity also comes with its own set of "everyday life" expectations for believers to engage with and its own influences on "subjectivity," implicit religion aims to exist still under this stream, intertwining itself with [practical] humanity more so than spirituality.

With the nature of true, unadulterated Christianity, the oneness of God, and the necessity of humility in the face of this God, implicit religiosity outside the realm of this God is not permissible. Therefore, being in concert with both hip-hop (that is, obtaining success and being acknowledged by other bodies within the hip-hop community) and Christianity presents the issue of the law of noncontradiction, whereby if the monolithic structure of Christianity does not permit other religious affiliations, hip-hop, in its full form, should not have a space. Even if it does have a space, it would eventually take up too much for Christianity to still be considered central to a person's life (as is demonstrated by the various deviations of many popular rap artists today).

This brings us to the phenomena that are the likes of Lecrae and NF. Not only have they obtained the communitarian[6] aspects

---

5. Clay, "Two Turntables and a Microphone," 24.

6. Hallan, *Short History of African Philosophy,* 15, quoting Mbiti.

of religiosity in the hip-hop community, but they also have the full respect of the Christian community. Lecrae rejects the title of Christian rapper and instead emphasizes time and again that his faith just manifests itself through his music. In this sense he criticizes both the groups he straddles between: the hip-hop culture that struggles to contextualize itself in the Christian purview despite claiming its tenets, as well as the Christians who limit Christianity to do's and don'ts, creating an exclusivity that perpetuates the marginalization of historically disadvantaged bodies.

Hip-hop for Christian rappers does not mean a rejection or distancing from the culture. In fact, Lecrae's and NF's lyrical topics demonstrate the opposite. From topics surrounding mental health, infidelity, and even some lyrics suggesting sexual prowess and flexing success, these prominent Christian rappers have not strayed at all far from the main body of hip-hop. Yet they have not sacrificed their tethers to the Christian God and continue expressing a gratefulness towards, or reliance on, Christ in their music.

In some sense, the flourishing of Christian rap within both the hip-hop and Christian communities represents progress towards Afrofuturist ideals for the diaspora. Not only does it express diasporic practices in ways that move beyond combatting historically oppressive forces, but it still acknowledges the effect of these historical disadvantages, their effects on their personal lives, and suggests ways in which to move toward the future (often entrenched in finding God). There are undeniable parallels between the evolution of hip-hop and the expansion of the Black community, Black culture, and Black identity. Today, Blackness exists and persists in many more spheres than it used to be able to, marking, not quite a period of prosperity, but a period of progress. The self-limiting within the Black community is still prevalent (you are not Black if you xyz, you can only be considered Black if you know unv) in some spheres but the existence and acceptance of Christian rap shows that even the most historically rigid structures of Black tradition are becoming more flexible and inclusive.

This is not to say finding Christ is the way to the Afrofuture (Christianity already plays a big role in the Black community), but rather, uniting fibers of the community that have remained distant from one another permits for the expansion of said community. In union, the Afrofuture can move into defining itself in spheres that Blackness has yet to penetrate. There is an undeniability to the way in which Christian rap makes hip-hop culture more palatable to those on its outskirts. If Afrofuturism does not aim to escape its present but rather move its various structures and groups together into Afrofuture, expanding its appeal may not be the worst move. Lecrae and NF have moved toward this expansion, and the community's ability to accept these new figures rings promising for an Afrofuture.

BIBLIOGRAPHY

Clay, Elonda. "Two Turntables and a Microphone: Turntablism, Ritual and implicit religion." *Culture and Religion* 10.1 (March 2009) 23–38.

Green, Emma. "Lecrae: 'Christians Have Prostituted Art to Give Answers.'" *The Atlantic*, October 6, 2014. https://www.theatlantic.com/entertainment/archive/2014/10/lecrae-christians-have-prostituted-art-to-give-answers/381103/.

Hallen, Barry. *A Short History of African Philosophy*. Bloomington: Indiana University Press, 2009.

King, Winston, and Lindsay Jones, eds. *Encyclopedia of Religion*. 2nd ed. Vol. 11. 12 vols. Detroit: Macmillan Reference USA, 2005.

Masci, David, et al. "Black Americans Are More Likely than Overall Public to Be Christian, Protestant." *Pew Research Center*, April 23, 2018. https://www.pewresearch.org/fact-tank/2018/04/23/black-americans-are-more-likely-than-overall-public-to-be-christian-protestant/.

McIntyre, Hugh. "Rapper NF Shockingly Hits No. 1 with his New Album 'Perception.'" *Forbes*, October 17, 2017. https://www.forbes.com/sites/hughmcintyre/2017/10/17/rapper-nf-shockingly-hits-no-1-with-his-new-album-perception/#617cbeeb7d26.

Power 106 Los Angeles. "Lecrae Doesn't Want to Be Labeled a Christian Rapper." https://www.youtube.com/watch?v=vJvbV4-pD6Q.

Williams, Juan. "Redefining What It Means to Be Black in America." 13 November, 2007, https://www.npr.org/templates/story/story.php?storyId=16260629.

Olu Omoyugbo

Hip-Hop through an Afrofuturist Lens

Breaking Down the Barriers

In the dingy, dimly lit basement in a suburban neighborhood south of Chicago's inner city, a young college dropout was laying the groundwork for a change that would dramatically shift the trajectory of rap, of hip-hop, and of black culture as a whole.

See, before it reached mainstream appeal and was a treasure trove of learnable "black culture" for white, upper-middle-class kids in the Midwest, hip-hop was a religion. A religion that found its footing in the underground and in the comfort of the ears of black and Hispanic youths of low-income neighborhoods who embraced the sound as something in which they could take pride in. But as the religion of hip-hop slowly started to crawl into the mainstream, it started to take shape and exist in a very one-dimensional space. A space that always felt congested with the basic build-a-rapper formula that only allowed the toxic masculinity-driven, poverty-filled, gangsterlicious, and gut-wrenching rhymes to squirm through on the *Billboard* charts. Hip-hop devolved into something that was stringent about the idea that you had to act a certain way and portray a certain image in order to be accepted as someone who could be marketed. The notion of black masculinity in rap is one that is often shrouded in a false sense of strength. And that was relatively the state of hip-hop, with the exclusion of A Tribe Called Quest and OutKast, until the emergence of Kanye West and his 2004 classic, *The College Dropout.*

Amidst his constant controversies and clashes with the paparazzi and the internet blogs, Kanye West is still a figure that is the cornerstone of the "evolved" rap we know today. The influence that his discography holds is one that is like no other when it comes to the religion of hip-hop. With his first album, he didn't try to portray himself as something that he wasn't. He didn't try to market himself as a drug-dealing thug who degrades women, hates homosexuals, and eliminates his competition. And this went against the benchmark rap had become accustomed to up until that point.

Dr. Dre's crudely named "Bitches Ain't Shit," which appeared on his 1992 album *The Chronic*, features one of the most famous and most quoted choruses of all time. In it, Snoop Dogg raps a refrain that articulates a vision of the sexual subservience of women to men. The magazine *Entertainment Weekly* gave the album an A+.

But the most essential element that mainstream hip-hop loved to bask its artist in, and what particularly set Kanye West apart from most of the rappers in his time, was the gangsterization of the artist's persona. At that point in time, the pinnacle of the rap game was 50 Cent and the G-Unit crew, a rap group that operated as more of a gang and involved some of the hardest gangsters in the game.

Yes, it's taxing and annoying. A form of pitting the good negro against the bad one, but it is, nevertheless, an important argument to point out. 50 Cent, by 2003 had already had a foothold on the rap game, and before him existed the drug-dealing Jay Z, Queensbridge affiliate Nas, and the late, great Notorious BIG. In terms of rap, there existed a real lack of diversity. And that was very understandable. The one-dimensional rap formula was working. You didn't even need to be part of a gang, or to have lived the life you talked about, you just had to put your life story on a good beat and with a good flow and you would be successful. In fact, even though 50 Cent dropped his *Get Rich or Die Tryin'* album with the song "High All the Time," he revealed in his 2005 book, *From Pieces to Weight*, that he never used drugs or drank liquor but rapped as if he did because artists were selling massive amounts of albums by doing so. Hip-hop before Kanye West was essentially entrapped in that notion of a need to be hard and strong all the time. *College Dropout* changed that. Kanye West allowed his vulnerability to permeate through his raps, as evidenced on "All Falls Down," the second track on the album. This was an awakening of the culture of hip-hop. West introduced a way in which you could still sell without having to have been a drug user, drug pusher, or gangbanger in your past life. On the song "Family Business," West directly addresses that toxic masculinity of always having to be tough and strong. *College Dropout* would go on to sell 4 million copies worldwide.

What can we learn from the adoption of Kanye West's *College Dropout* by hip-hop heads around the world? Is it possible in a Afrofuturist religion of hip-hop to show vulnerability, the ability to show emotions greater than just the need to demean women, sell drugs, and stack your body count? Yes.

In fact, an acceptance of difference is something that an Afrofuturist philosophy desperately needs. More often than not, black culture is subjugated into boxes that don't allow for much deviation, unless we are talking about female rap.

Rap, as much as it pains me to say, is built on the oversexualization of women. Misogyny runs rampant in rap, and it is even expected of rappers that they will disrespect women. But amidst the toxicity of male rappers and their sexist ideas of female exploitation rose the voices of female rappers who championed acceptance of body, gender, and sexuality and a diversity in the range of topics that were able to be talked about.

In 1996, Lil' Kim announced herself to the world with her raunchy and in-your-face *Hard Core* album, with a cover that was scandalous enough to make a Christian conservative mother of two from Idaho faint. Sexual positivity is an important facet to feminism in rap because it takes back the power of sex from men. For the women who listened to Lil' Kim, they could be proud to want sex, to talk about sex, and to not be subjected to humiliation for having sex. This celebration of sex and self-fulfillment continues on the song "Queen Bitch." A flip on the male narrative where male rappers often describe their sexcapades with women as something they are owed and talk about the women in a way that classifies them as second-class citizens, Lil' Kim talks about how "buffoons" are eating her pussy, which can be viewed as an allusion to the power she holds as the alpha dog—a changing of the gender roles. This same semblance of female rap can still be felt today with the rise and success of Cardi B, a "regular, degular shmegular girl from the Bronx."[1] She, like Lil' Kim, takes control over her own sexuality and embraces ways in which she has used her body in order to "finesse and hustle."[2] She represents femininity in the modern age because she doesn't conform to the societal ideals of what a woman has to be. In the song "Get Up 10," she takes pride in her fake boobs. She also takes on the role of the male boss and turns it on its head, in the song "She Bad." Cardi B and Lil' Kim represent the ability to create something that doesn't necessarily fit into the mold of what being a woman is usually thought of as being, and in them doing this they create a new way of thinking, a new lens that opens the door for a wider reaching variety of female experiences.

This embracing of difference in female rap is what allowed for rappers like Lauryn Hill and Janelle Monáe to exist in the same realm as Lil' Kim and Cardi B and still be just as successful. For Lauryn Hill, rather than flipping and deconstructing gender roles, what separates her from most other rappers is an allowance for a feeling of vulnerability, especially in her only solo album, *The Miseducation of Lauryn Hill*. In the song "Ex-Factor," she raps about her willingness to change who she was in order to appeal to a man who doesn't necessarily even like her. This all culminates in her reflecting in her chorus on the insanity of her lover pushing her away while simultaneously desiring her to stay. This line, and this song in particular, shows an unmasking of what it is to truly try to be a strong woman, while still being able to circumvent the trappings of a toxic relationship. This exploration of being a woman who is strong yet vulnerable continues in the song, "Doo Wop (That Thing)," where she shares her advice on how not to fall in that trap of expecting too much from a man when they show you time and time again that they are

1. Porcelain, "How Social Media Allowed," 1.
2. Iasimone, "Cardi B on Being a Feminist," 1.

not worthy of the effort you put in for them. She then includes lines showing that this isn't something she is speaking just to speak, but something she has personally gone through, once again showing her vulnerability and the ability to relate to people who listen to her. She represents Afrofuturism because she dismantles the notion of the strong black woman trope, and allows herself to appear weak and open. Her album would later go on to sell 8 million copies in the US alone, and also win the Grammy Award for Album of the Year, showing just how integral female rap is to a change in perspective.

But in the modern age, Noname best reflects what a true Afrofuturist philosophy of hip-hop can be—a combination of the two that portrays Noname as a person the listeners can most closely relate to. This can also be felt with her album, *Room 25*. Like Lauryn Hill, she allows herself to be emotionally vulnerable and to show herself in a light most of her listeners can relate to, while still being able to portray the brashness and self-assertion of both Lil' Kim and Cardi B. In the first song on the album, "Self," she details the traits of a bad man in the second verse. Here she shows vulnerability as she talks about a man who is constantly letting her down and how she often feels when her man disappoints her yet again. But the sentiment of emptiness which starts the verse is very quickly transitioned out of, and the mood switches to one of audacious and borderline raunchy women empowerment. In a song that only lasts a minute and thirty-seven seconds, she is able to balance a duality of confidence and vulnerability—meeting the common ground of rap that can propel us into a truly Afrofuturist philosophy of rap.

Feminism in rap encapsulates the ability to break down barriers and an openness to deconstruct the normalities which society creates. Rappers like Lil' Kim, Cardi B, Lauryn Hill, and Noname epitomize what Monica Miller preaches in her book, *Religion and Hip Hop*. Miller believes that in a truly Afrofuturist world, "rather than rejecting the radical potential already present in black popular culture, increased engagement is needed, a type of engagement that embraces the myriad of ways in which 'difference' itself is lived."[3] They represent an ability to deviate from the norm while still being

3. Miller, *Religion and Hip Hop*, 43.

able to be embraced. They don't have to put themselves inside a box to be accepted, and they don't have to follow a particular formula that tells them they have to feel a certain way, talk a certain way, and act a certain way. To perfectly define what an Afrofuturist philosophy of hip-hop can be you have to take away the boxes that already exist in Afrodiasporic philosophy of hip-hop today. Rap doesn't have to be rooted in capitalistic greed or the need to be overly masculine in order to present a facade. This is what female rap does well, and what male rap has the potential to do well. Because once you remove labels related to what a rapper can be, you create sounds that are innovative and futuristic. You create artists like the pink polo-rocking Kanye West, or the dress-wearing Young Thug, who contribute greatly to the advancement of rap in general. If we didn't have a Kanye West, we wouldn't have a Drake or a Big Sean, and if we didn't have a Young Thug, we would not have had a Lil Baby or Gunna. An open approach and willingness to change is what can move an idea forward. The change that an Afrofuturist policy needs is one where no box is needed to define how an artist can rap like or what an artist can look like.

This willingness to do away with stereotyping what a rapper can be will push black culture, as a whole, forward. Once we learn to embrace black rappers who suffer from mental health issues and allow them to show emotions that range beyond than the usual "get money, fuck bitches" attitude, we can open discussion to mental health in the black community and work together and try to fix that problem. Hip-hop is seen as the gateway to black culture; if we can learn to advance hip-hop, black culture as a whole will definitely benefit.

WORKS CITED PAGE

Belicazar, Cardi. "Cardi B & YG—She Bad." genius.com/Cardi-b-and-yg-she-bad-lyrics.

———. "Cardi B—Get Up 10." genius.com/Cardi-b-get-up-10-lyrics.

Hill, Lauryn. "Lauryn Hill—Doo Wop (That Thing)." genius.com/Lauryn-hill-doo-wop-that-thing-lyrics.

———. "Lauryn Hill—Ex-Factor." genius.com/Lauryn-hill-ex-factor-lyrics.

Iasimone, Ashley. "Cardi B on Being a Feminist: 'Anything a Man Can Do, I Can Do.'" *Billboard*, February 12, 2018. www.billboard.com/articles/columns/hip-hop/8099087/cardi-b-feminist-stripping-intervie w-i-d-magazine.

Miller, Monica R. *Religion and Hip Hop*. New York: Routledge, 2013.

Porcelain, Feraud. "How Social Media Allowed Cardi B to Go from Being a Regular, Degular, Schmegular Girl to the Top of. . ." *Medium*, April 22, 2018. medium.com/rta902/how-social-media-allowed-cardi-b-to-go-from-being-a-regular-degular-schmegular-girl-to-the-top-of-230f8a9f7d67.

Warner, Fatimah. "Noname—Self." genius.com/Noname-self-lyrics.